AURA GARDEN GUIDES

Dorothée Wächter

Plants for Shady Places

Practical advice on choosing suitable plants, preparing
the soil and planting

AURA

Aura Garden Guides

Plants for Shady Places

Dorothée Wächter

German-language edition and photographs
Schattenplätze im Garten: Die besten Pflanzen: Gestalten und Pflegen
© BLV Verlagsgesellschaft, Munich 2001

Translation: Andrew Shackleton

English-language edition © 2004
Aura Books plc

Produced by:
Transedition Limited for Aura Books, Bicester

Design and picture layout by:
Studio Schübel, Munich; Anton Walter and
DTP-Design Walter, Gündelfingen

Editing and text layout by:
Asgard Publishing Services, Leeds

Typesetting:
Organ Graphic, Abingdon

10 9 8 7 6 5 4 3 2 1
Printed in Dubai

ISBN 1 903938 51 1

Photo credits:
Adams: 28, 33, 39b, 46b, 52b, 57b, 63b, 64t,
69b; Baumjohann: 91; Borstell: 2/3, 4, 9, 12, 13,
14, 15b, 17, 20, 22, 26, 27, 29, 30, 31, 32, 34,
35, 36, 41t, 44t, b, 47t, b, 49t, 53bl, br, 55b, 57t
58t, b, 62t, 66b, 69t, b, 70b, 71, 73, 82, 84b, 86,
87, 88, 93, 94; Brand: 8, 11, 40t, 42b, 43b, 53t,
56t, 67b, 76, 83; Bühl: 90b; Fischer, E.: 6, 23,
74; Fischer, G.: 85; Hagen: 61t, 62b; Redeleit:
84t; Reinhard: 7, 10, 15t, 24, 38b, 39t, 40b, 45t,
50t, 54b, 56b, 59t, 60b, 66t, 67t, 72, 75, 78t, b,
80, 90t; Romeis: 25, 48, 65t; Ruckszio: 42t, 51,
55t, 70t, 77; Seidl: 38t, 41b, 43t, 46t, 49b, 50b,
52t, 54t, 59b, 60t, 61b, 63t, 64b, 65b, 68.

Drawings: Heidi Janiček

Contents

The case for shade

Shady places may pose problems for gardeners, simply because the requirements are different from those of sunny places in terms of design, maintenance and the choice of plants. Yet shady places also have many advantages.

Sun and shade are opposites. The sun has usually been seen in a positive light, sometimes even to the extent of being worshipped, while shade has been viewed in purely negative terms. However, gardeners blessed with a shady garden have the opportunity to rid themselves of this unhelpful 'black-and-white' attitude.

After all, there is such a broad range of plants available for growing in the shade, including almost every kind of plant, with an infinite variety of flowers in every colour and form – as is amply demonstrated in this book (see page 37 ff.).

The many garden flowers from shaded forests were what provided the inspiration for the woodland garden movement. This movement was begun by William Robinson, an Irish gardener who had come to London in the 1860s. Robinson rejected the formality of previous generations, suggesting that a garden should almost be a piece of the countryside. He advocated naturalising bulbs and planting groups of perennials informally in a jumble of colours, rather than in straight lines.

At the beginning of the gardening season, shady places offer beautifully romantic spring settings. In the summer they can provide a gorgeous display of colourful flowers combined with elegant greenery. Then, as the year draws to a close, they form the backdrop for a gentle Indian summer punctuated by fiery autumn colours.

The advantages of shade

Shade provides a relatively temperate microclimate that in general supports easy-care plantings. The ground may not dry out so quickly, providing plants with more stable conditions.

On a wooden bench around the foot of a tree, you can enjoy cooling shade at any time of day.

And a canopy of tree foliage increases the humidity levels, creating the optimum conditions for growth.

Shady places often require less work in summer, simply because they may need less watering during times of drought. The humus-rich soil and the reduced evaporation mean that the roots have a more stable supply of moisture. Add a layer of ground-cover plants to the equation, and even less general maintenance is required.

◀ Rhododendrons open their glorious red blooms beneath the shade of trees, while ferns unfurl their fresh-green fronds.

Take a walk through the woods and look at the different plant communities to be found there. Such models will provide much inspiration for gardening in shady places.

Shade as opposed to sun doesn't mean that the ground is totally deprived of light at all times of the day or night. On the contrary, only a couple of hours without sunlight can make a place seem shady. The resulting interplay of light makes for variety of form. The varied light conditions bring the colours and shapes to life, adding an element of drama to the scene.

Shade in the garden may be pleasant for people as well as for plants. In the heat of the summer sun, the cool of the shade invites us to rest and relax.

A shady garden provides yet one more advantage. If there's too much shade, all you need to do is prune a few branches off a large shrub to provide extra light for the flowers. In a sunny garden, by contrast, much effort may be required to create just a few pockets of shade that in turn require a good deal of patience before they develop into enough shade to be worth their while.

Different kinds of shade

Not all kinds of shade are the same. It is in fact possible to distinguish between several different types of shade on the basis of the amount of light that is available: light shade, dappled shade, half-shade and deep shade. Moreover, the dampness of the ground will similarly affect the kinds of plants that can be grown. So you can also make a distinction between dry shade, damp shade and wet shade.

Light shade

Light shade describes a situation where only some of the sun's rays are blocked and plenty of light can still reach the plants. Light shade occurs in the wild beneath trees with thin leaves such as birches. It can also be found under an awning or a piece of coarse netting.

In the spring, well before any leaves start to appear on deciduous trees, the ground beneath them may be covered with a rich and colourful carpet of flowers such as Scilla siberica.

Dappled shade

Dappled shade describes a gentle alternation between sunlight and shade such as may be found under a tree with an open crown that lets plenty of light through among the leaves. A pergola or an avenue of trees will similarly provide dappled shade. Such a situation provides all kinds of lively design possibilities, taking full advantage of the gentle interplay of light and shade.

Half-shade

Half-shade is used to describe an area that lies in both the sun and the shade at different times of day. Half-shaded flower beds are particularly desirable if they get plenty of sun during the morning and late afternoon, but are fully protected from direct sunlight during the heat of the day.

Deep shade

Deep shade is the kind of shade that is to be found beneath large, mature trees, or in gardens surrounded by high walls, or where a large building cuts out the sun for much of the day. There will be a much smaller range of plants to

Granny's bonnets (Aquilegia vulgaris) *provides a lively display of flowers that range in colour from red and violet through to white. New seedlings bring yet more colours into the equation.*

choose from in such situations, but still enough to create a varied display.

Dry shade

In the wild, trees with dense foliage tend to create a lot of dry shade. In a garden, on the other hand, the main reason for dry shade may be the proximity of buildings, which allow too little water or moisture to reach the soil. In addition, overhanging roofs or walls physically prevent the rain from falling on the ground.

It's difficult for plants to get a proper foothold in such dry areas of the garden unless a little irrigation of some sort is provided. This in turn will encourage the roots to spread so that they can absorb more water and nutrients from deeper layers in the soil.

9

Damp or wet shade

Moisture tends to collect in the soil in the neighbourhood of streams, over impermeable layers or where the water table is high. These situations are common in the wild, and there are plenty of plant species that are well adapted to the poor light conditions and the excess water that are characteristic of such locations.

Artificial methods are often needed to create similar areas in a garden, where sufficient moisture will then be available to satisfy the requirements of moisture-loving shade plants such as ferns or primroses (*Primula*).

A fragrant pot-pourri of white flowers made up of wild garlic (Allium ursinum), *sweet woodruff* (Galium odoratum) *and lily-of-the-valley* (Convallaria majalis)

Harmony versus competition

If you look at a shaded plant community in the wild – in a woodland, for example – you will find trees and bulb plants, bushes and ferns, all living together in harmony, each layer being occupied by a different set of plants.

The smallest plants take advantage of the early spring before the leaves appear on the trees, coming into flower, feeling the benefit of the spring sunshine and collecting nutrients from the soil. Soon after, the ferns open their fronds, while the grasses push up fresh green stems.

Later on, as the foliage forms on the trees, the undergrowth becomes cool and shady, and now the taller perennials and ground-cover plants come into their own.

It has of course taken thousands of years for this kind of harmony to develop in the wild

To produce the same effect in a garden, and to develop an intricate community of plants,

The woodland spring is marked by blue ribbons of flowers such as Corydalis flexuosa *and* Chionodoxa.

requires a high degree of knowledge and sensitivity. For, quite apart from the search for light, every plant is in competition with its neighbours in the bid to find sufficient water and nutrients.

The plant roots too need to be ordered at different levels, just like the stems and trunks. If you plant trees and shrubs, their roots need to penetrate deep down into the soil to leave space above them for those of bulb plants and herbaceous perennials. If shrubs develop shallow roots, it becomes difficult for herbs and smaller plants to gain a foothold.

If trees with shallow roots are already present – pines or birches, for example – then there are various gardening tricks that you can use for getting round the problem. You can, for example, add an extra layer of soil and plant strong ground-cover plants that will quickly fill the area around the trees. Or alternatively you could work with ivy (*Hedera*) or periwinkle (*Vinca*). If these climbers are planted around the tree, their creeping shoots will quickly spread to cover the whole area.

However, apart from these various gardening ruses, the best way to plant in the shade is to imitate the patterns that can already be found in the wild. Then you will be assured of quick success, and a minimum of maintenance will be required to keep your shady places looking good.

at a glance

- Shady gardens provide a delight all of their own, and in the summer they provide a cool haven for relaxation.

- Shady gardens are generally low-maintenance. Less watering is required, for example, as the ground dries out more slowly.

- Shade provides a whole range of different lighting conditions, and these also change with the march of the seasons, with the height of the sun and the foliage on the trees. The type of shade will also vary depending on the degree of light penetration and the proximity of walls and buildings.

- A distinction can be made between light shade, dappled shade, half-shade and deep shade.

- The soil conditions are yet another important factor. One can, for example, distinguish between dry shade in the shelter of large trees and damp shade in the neighbourhood of ponds and streams.

11

Design ideas for shady places

This chapter contains ten different design models, each with a particular theme, to provide some ideas and suggestions for designing a garden in the shade.

The main focus of these garden designs is of course the plants themselves, with their interesting flowers and foliage.

Some plantings will provide the main focus in the spring, summer or autumn, while evergreens will help to enliven the winter scene. Other designs will focus on leaf textures or on specific shapes. Others again will focus on the location and maintenance of the site: moisture-loving shade plants, easy-care plantings and long-flowering displays.

A plan of action

Before you go on to consider the plants themselves, the first thing you need to do is to plan everything out. Even if you simply intend to follow one of the design suggestions in this book, it is advisable to make a sketch of the area to be planted

◀ *Behind the large, distinctively heart-shaped leaves of the* Hosta, *the taller* Astilbe *sports dense sprays of strawberry-pink flowers.*

and to think again carefully about the plants you want to choose. The following points are essential to consider when designing a garden:

- Think about plant communities in the wild that you find particularly pleasing. This will help your design to look really natural.

- Introduce plenty of variation into your plans. Ground-cover plants on their own are easy to look after, but they are vulnerable to the same pests and diseases.

- You should include at least some plants for every season. Bear in mind that a few bulb plants will flower in the late winter, and that evergreens can enhance the dullest winter shade.

- Try to vary the height of plants so as to give structure and form to the design. You could imitate a painting by carefully grading the plant heights with the tall plants at the back. Or you could create gaps that provide tantalising glimpses of other areas of the

Feathery fern fronds contrast nicely with the darker, more well-defined leaves of Rodgersia.

garden. Or you could use taller plants to hide the less desirable items such as the compost heap.

- As a general rule, smaller plants should go at the front with taller ones at the back, so that nothing is hidden. But you also need to take the flowering times into account. For example, small spring-flowering perennials and bulb plants could be placed at the back so that, as the leaves wilt over the summer, they will be hidden by taller summer and autumn perennials.

Mosses tend to grow in damp, shady places and can add an extra dimension to a planting. These decorative cushions can be deliberately sited on a rock or statue. There are at least two ways of doing this. You can place the object in wet grass in the shade for several weeks, or alternatively you can paint or spray it with yoghurt or buttermilk so that the extra protein will encourage the formation of algae and mosses.

- Don't just choose flowering plants – include some decorative foliage plants too. Ferns, grasses and large-leaved perennials provide havens of rest and offset the beauty of the flowers.
- Lighter-coloured leaves and flowers are to be preferred in the shade. They catch the light and make even the shadiest corner brighter. Leaves with white or yellow variegations are similarly desirable.
- Try to build certain patterns into your design so as to create a sense of unity. By repeating similar colours in different areas, for example, you can create bridges between features that are otherwise unconnected.
- Contrasts can be used to similar effect. The colours and shapes of leaves can be very helpful here, creating links between neighbouring plants.
- Allow just enough space between plants so that they grow together over the first two years. The result will look good and will reduce the amount of maintenance required.
- Add a few accessories and decorative items to the display. Bright surfaces will provide extra visual interest. Garden furniture or zinc containers are ideal for this purpose. Glass balls or even crystals from an ancient chandelier (the sort of thing you might find at a car boot sale) can add a romantic glint to the shade and arouse curiosity.
- Try to integrate your shady areas with the rest of the garden. It can be difficult, for example, to establish a lawn or ground-cover plants under the shade of a large tree, so this may be the ideal place for siting a garden path.

Rhododendrons play an important role in a spring garden, creating a colourful backdrop to a whole panoply of spring-flowering perennials.

- Place a garden seat in the shade, where you can sit during the heat of a summer day, and you will soon learn to love this shady spot.

A medley of spring flowers

Shade plays a particularly important role in the first weeks of spring, because it is where the first flowers start to bring colour to the scene.

Sweet violet (*Viola odorata*), for example, doesn't follow the calendar, but simply waits until the temperature starts to rise. It only has to get a little warmer, even in January, and the first purple-coloured flowers can be

The purple and pink flowers of the spring-flowering pea (Lathyrus vernus) *combine with other shade-loving plants to form a decorative carpet.*

glimpsed amid the fresh-green leaves. Snowdrops (*Galanthus*)

and winter aconite (*Eranthis hyemalis*) are similarly impatient to flower.

This is scarcely surprising, since the main aim of these plants isn't so much to steal the show as to take advantage of the first light of the season before the leaves grow on the trees. Most of these low-growing perennials form carpets of leaves over the years. However, many of them die back at the beginning of summer.

A basket and two old lamps come into their own between the cranesbill (Geranium) *and the ferns.*

15

You therefore need to be very careful when choosing a site for a spring bed. You need to be able to find access to it easily in the late winter in order to enjoy the first flowers, but on the other hand it shouldn't be too much in the foreground, as some of the plants will tend to leave bare patches as they die back for a well-deserved summer rest.

Planting suggestion

This sample design contains classic spring plants that inter-weave to form a carpet. A whole variety of typical spring flowers have been blended into a single unit that will provide flowers from January to June.

The aptly named ostrich fern or shuttlecock fern (*Matteuccia struthiopteris*) looks really good in a spring bed, but this plant can unfortunately be very invasive. To avoid such a problem, you could dig out a large hole and place a large paint can in it with the bottom cut out. If you plant the fern in here, it will be unable to spread. You can, however, divide it and plant the offspring somewhere else in the same bed.

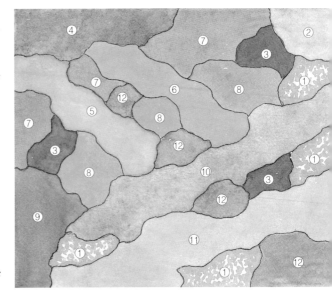

The individual species that have been chosen are inter-spersed so as to give the bed a really natural feel, while the varied height of the plants lends a definite structure to the layout as a whole.

The colours of the plants have also been matched. Spring is symbolised by the colour blue. In those immortal words of Robert Schumann's song *Er ist's* ('Spring is here'): 'Spring lets its blue ribbon flutter through the air again.'

So blue shades play a major role in this design. If you have a penchant for these colours,

1 *Galanthus nivalis* (common snowdrop)

2 *Hyacinthoides hispanica* (Spanish bluebell)

3 *Aquilegia vulgaris* (granny's bonnet)

4 *Matteuccia struthiopteris* (ostrich fern)

5 *Galium odoratum* (sweet woodruff)

6 *Pulmonaria angustifolia* 'Azurea' (blue cowslip)

7 *Lathyrus vernus* (spring-flowering pea)

8 *Erythronium dens-canis* (dog's-tooth violet)

9 *Brunnera macrophylla*

10 *Omphalodes verna* (blue-eyed Mary)

11 *Anemone sylvestris* (snowdrop windflower)

12 *Corydalis cava*

hen spring is the time to enjoy hem. The darker the shade under the trees becomes, the paler the blue becomes and the fewer blue flowers are to be found in this part of the garden.

From a horticultural point of view, you should leave plenty of space in the first year or so for ground-cover plants such as blue-eyed Mary, blue cowslip and sweet woodruff, so that as they spread out they don't push out smaller plants such as the dog's-tooth violet and spring-flowering pea. Perennials and bulb plants like a humus-rich soil, which can be produced by mulching with leaf compost.

An alternative spring planting suggestion, based around yellow flowers:

- *Eranthis hyemalis* (winter aconite)
- *Doronicum orientale* (leopard's bane)
- *Euphorbia amygdaloides* var. *robbiae*
- *Erythronium* 'Pagoda'
- *Primula veris* (cowslip)
- *Trillium luteum* (yellow woodlily)
- *Uvularia grandiflora* (bellwort)
- *Waldsteinia*

Decorative foliage

Any gardener who has worked with grasses and ferns will have given at least some thought to the use of decorative foliage. For many years its beauties lay mostly unrecognised, but it has recently come more into the limelight again.

Foliage can make for some wonderfully contrasted and varied designs, whose visual effect will also last for very much longer than any flower compositions can possibly do. Foliage plants also provide a restful accompaniment to flowering plants.

Decorative foliage designs can be based on a variety of aspects.

The sample design overleaf is mainly based on the colour of the leaves.

Green is not only the main colour of foliage, but effectively forms the basis for all plant life. This is because the chlorophyll that is responsible for the green colour is essential to the process of photosynthesis, by which plants obtain energy from sunlight.

However, this doesn't mean that the chlorophyll – and with it the green colour – is evenly distributed in the foliage. It may be overlaid with other colours, or indeed absent from some parts of the leaves, creating a variety of colours and patterns in the process.

Hellebores, anemones and plantain lilies (Hosta) *combine in visual harmony.*

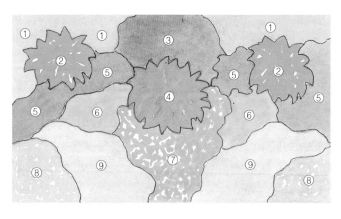

1 *Polygonatum odoratum* 'Variegatum' (Solomon's seal)

2 *Hosta undulata* var. *undulata*

3 *Helleborus foetidus* (stinking hellebore)

4 *Hosta undulata* 'Albomarginata' syn. *H.* 'Thomas Hogg'

5 *Dicentra formosa* 'Alba'

6 *Pulmonaria* 'Sissinghurst White'

7 *Lamium maculatum* 'White Nancy' (spotted deadnettle)

8 *Carex ornithopoda* 'Variegata'

9 *Astilbe glaberrima* var. *saxatilis*

Planting suggestion

This sample design concentrates on plants with white-variegated foliage. Apart from their decorative value, such plants will help to bring more light into the picture. Because any white surfaces reflect the light, they will bring much-needed brightness to parts of the shade.

Providing extra light for decorative foliage

A white garden chair or silver balls are enough to brighten up a flower bed in the shade without detracting from the display itself. Zinc containers can have a similar effect when they catch the light.

The plants are placed roughly symmetrically across a vertical axis. The Solomon's seal at the back presents a tall backdrop from early in the year. Immediately in front of it, the stinking hellebore (*Helleborus foetidus*) bears green-coloured flowers, followed later on in the year by the *Pulmonaria* 'Sissinghurst White', with its white flowers and silvery-flecked leaves. This close relative of our native lungwort soon grows to form a dense layer of greenery.

The spotted deadnettle carries on the dialogue, its round, patterned leaves edged with white in this particular cultivar. The long blades of the *Carex ornithopoda* 'Variegata', a decorative form of sedge, have similar white edges that in this case give the effect of stripes. The low-growing *Astilbe* spreads out between the deadnettle and the clumps of sedge-grass. In the summer this plant becomes covered with a veil of soft-pink flowers, creating a visual resting point.

In the background, the blue-grey foliage and white flowers of *Dicentra formosa* 'Alba' set off the stronger patterns of the *Hosta* plants. Of these, the *H. undulata* var. *undulata* on either side creates swirling patterns with the bold designs on its wavy leaves, while the stately *H. undulata* 'Albomarginata' occupies the centre of the display.

The whole bed will provide a glorious display of foliage right through until the late autumn.

Yellow for warmth
If you feel that white is a cold colour, then you could use yellow instead. There are yellow-variegated forms of both *Hosta* and deadnettle, while *Carex ornithopoda* 'Variegata' could be replaced with the gold-variegated *Hakonechloa macra* 'Aureola'. Other plants might then include *Euonymus fortunei* 'Emerald 'n' Gold' and yellow-variegated forms of ivy (*Hedera helix*). The yellow flowers of lady's mantle (*Alchemilla mollis*) and Welsh poppy (*Meconopsis cambrica*) continue the yellow theme.

Decorative foliage plants

Common/botanical name	Height (cm/in)	Description of foliage	Flowering time/colour
Lady's mantle (*Alchemilla mollis*)	30–80 (12–32)	grey-green, limp, large (13 ×15 cm / 5 × 6 in), very hairy, morning dew-drops, good linking colour	June; if cut back after flowering, will bloom again in August / yellowish-green
Wild ginger (*Asarum europaeum*)	5–15 (2–6)	shiny dark green, long stems, broadly ovate (3 × 6 cm / 1 × 2.5 in), evergreen	April to June / brownish outside, dark red inside
Hard fern (*Blechnum spicant*)	25–75 (10–30)	dark green, matt, leathery, indented, up to 4 cm (1.5 in) wide, forming a regular rosette in young plants; narrow fronds ripen in summer, growing up to 75 cm (30 in) in height, and are evergreen.	—
Chiastophyllum oppositifolium	10–15 (4–6)	light green, firm and roundish, serrated, succulent	June to July / yellow
Corydalis cheilanthifolia	20–30 (8–12)	brownish green, pinnate, fern-like, striking red autumn colouring	May to June / yellow
Tufted hair grass (*Deschampsia cespitosa*)	50–150 (20–60)	flat with sharp keel, rough on top, over-hanging; forms dense clumps, doesn't proliferate; good for cut leaves	June to August / green at first, later yellow
Helleborus argutifolius	40–60 (16–24)	succulent, tripartite, sharply serrated, evergreen; stem-forming species	March to April / yellowish-green
Dame's violet/Sweet rocket (*Hesperis matronalis*)	60–80 (24–32)	dark green, serrated, heart-shaped triangular, lanceolate above	May to June / violet or white, with evening scent of violet
Himalayan blue poppy (*Meconopsis betonicifolia*)	90–120 (35–48)	long stems, oval to heart-shaped, serrated, rough with brownish hairs	June to July / sky-blue with yellow stamens
Fringecups (*Tellima grandiflora*)	50–60 (20–24)	roundish to heart-shaped, long stems, organised in rosettes	May to June / white to green

This planting highlights the marked contrasts in texture between the foliage of three different plants – from the deeply furrowe[d], leathery leaves of the white-variegated Hosta *to the soft but firm fronds of the royal fern* (Osmunda regalis) *and the enormous, shield-like leaves of* Astilboides tabularis *(syn.* Rodgersia tabularis).

The interplay of textures

Every leaf feels subtly different to the touch. The foliage of lady's mantle (*Alchemilla mollis*), for example, feels soft and fluffy, while the grey-blue leaves of *Hosta sieboldiana* 'Elegans' feel dull and waxy, and the fronds of the hart's-tongue fern (*Asplenium scolopendrium*) are smooth and regular.

The surface of a leaf is one of its most salient features. We can perceive the surface details by both sight and touch. This outer layer can vary enormously. It may be dull or shiny, or perhaps thick and waxy, which sometimes protects the leaf from evaporation. Sometimes it may be covered with a velvety or silvery sheen made up of tiny hairs that help to increase transpiration. This function is not required in the shade, so there are only a few silvery-leaved plants on offer.

There may be chalky deposits on a leaf that make the surface seem rough. Leaves may also vary in their thickness, or in th[e] way the edges are formed or t[he] veins run through them. Som[e] leaves may be deeply furrowe[d]. All these variations can make for interesting contrasts of texture.

The design suggestion that follows makes full use of the interplay between a whole variety of textures, not to mention various leaf colours, [to] create a lively display made u[p] of interesting perennials, grass[es] and shrubs.

Planting suggestion

The main fulcrum at the back of the display is the rhododendron bush, with its long, shiny, dark-green leaves. The soft, fluffy foliage of the neighbouring foxgloves (*Digitalis purpurea*) makes for variety, while their columns of flowers create a lively contrast with the voluptuous blooms of the rhododendron. The pink of the foxgloves blends more gently with the violet tones of the giant bellflower (*Campanula latifolia*). If you want a more restful effect, then you could choose one of the white-flowered 'Alba' varieties.

Also at the back, the painted fern (*Athyrium nipponicum* var. *pictum*) provides a lively medley of colours and shapes,

while the diagonal band of lady's mantle in the centre acts as a visual focus. In the middle, the red-brown foliage and purple flowers of *Heuchera micrantha* 'Palace Purple' form a link between the various beds.

To the left of the display, the rougher feel of the *Brunnera macrophylla* combines with the bright-green foliage of the bugle (*Ajuga reptans*), while to the right the gold-variegated blades of the *Hakonechloa macra* 'Aureola' are in stark contrast to the frizzy cushions of the *Saxifraga* 'Blütenteppich'.

Summer pruning

The plants in these beds should be thoroughly pruned just once in high summer. Cutting back the foxgloves stops them seeding too much, and generally prolongs the life of the biennial leaf rosettes. The lady's mantle should be cut back almost to ground level after the first flowering is over.

The fresh growth of leaves will give these plants a much cleaner look for the second half of the summer, and one or two of the plants will probably bloom a second time round.

1 *Rhododendron yakushimanum* hybrid
2 *Digitalis purpurea* (foxglove)
3 *Campanula latifolia* (giant bellflower)
4 *Brunnera macrophylla*
5 *Alchemilla mollis* (lady's mantle)
6 *Ajuga reptans* (bugle)
7 *Saxifraga* 'Blütenteppich'
8 *Hakonechloa macra* 'Aureola'
9 *Heuchera micrantha* 'Palace Purple'
10 *Athyrium nipponicum* var. *pictum* (painted fern)

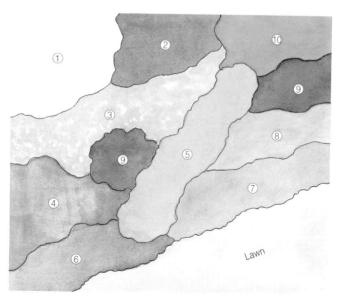

Shapes and patterns

There are lots of different shapes in a garden – those of the leaves, flowers and sprays, as well as the whole shape of each plant. Plant profiles also play an important role in garden design.

The interlinking of both similar and contrasting shapes brings the whole display to life. The interplay of patterns creates a drama all of its own that enlivens the whole display, almost as though a red thread were being pulled all the way through it.

These box bushes have been pruned and shaped so as to imitate the pattern of the rhododendron flowers.

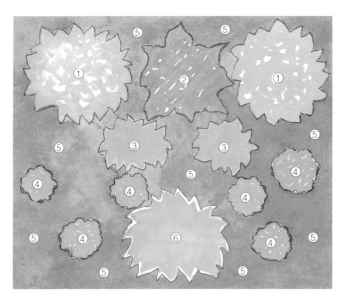

Planting suggestion

'Round shapes' is the motto f this particular design. The tw hydrangeas at the back set th ball rolling, so to speak, with their spherical flower sprays. The longevity of these gloriou blooms is further enhanced b

1 *Hydrangea macrophylla*

2 *Dryopteris affinis* syn. *D. affinis bc*

3 *Hosta* 'Halcyon'

4 *Buxus sempervivens* (spherically pruned box)

5 *Astilbe chinensis* var. *pumila*

6 *Hosta* 'Francee'

he fact that, even as the colours start to fade, the flowers continue to radiate beauty. The spherical cut of the box bushes carries on the 'circular' theme, as does the rounded foliage of the three *Hosta* plants.

These flattish leaves then find a contrast in the deeply dissected foliage of the *Astilbe* and the light, feathery fronds of the *Dryopteris affinis*. During the summer months, the upright flower sprays of the *Hosta* and *Astilbe* add yet more interest to the scene.

This design is easy to maintain because the *Astilbe* spreads quickly to form a thick carpet that keeps the weeds firmly at bay. There remains the business of pruning the box, which needs to be shaped once a year to keep its spherical form. This, together with the evergreen fronds of the fern, provides decorative interest in winter.

This design demonstrates that an interesting shade planting can be achieved with the minimum of plant species. Ornamentals and ground-cover plants complement each other very well, and the resulting harmony and balance lend an air of peace and calm to the whole display.

Slug-resistant plants

Slugs and snails are the biggest enemy of ornamental foliage plants, producing unsightly holes in the loveliest of leaves. Plantain lilies (*Hosta*) are particularly vulnerable to their predations.

The following shade plants have proved resistant to slugs and snails:

- monkshood (*Aconitum*)
- baneberry (*Actaea*)
- *Astilbe*
- *Brunnera macrophylla*
- foxglove (*Digitalis*)
- *Epimedium*
- sweet woodruff (*Galium odoratum*)
- hellebore (*Helleborus*)
- Jacob's ladder (*Polemonium*).

Beautiful ornamentals and ground-cover plants	
Group	**Plants**
Ground cover	*Ajuga* (bugle), *Duchesnea indica* (mock strawberry), *Pachysandra terminalis*, *Pulmonaria* (lungwort), *Tiarella* (foamflower), *Waldsteinia*
Ornamentals	*Angelica gigas*, *Kirengeshoma palmata*, *Matteuccia struthiopteris* (ostrich fern), *Astilboides tabularis* syn. *Rodgersia tabularis*

The following species and varieties of **Hosta** are considered more resistant: H. 'Big Daddy', H. 'Blue Angel', H. *fortunei* var. *aureomarginata*, H. 'Frances Williams', H. Tardiana hybrids and H. *tardiflora*.

Some varieties of Hosta grow into quite impressive plants that add a touch of beauty to the shadiest path.

Lady's eardrops (Fuchsia magellanica) *provides a magnificent display of pendant blooms throughout the summer, right up until the first autumn frosts.*

Summer moods

The more shady a garden is, the more you tend to long for bright flowers in the summer. Given the wide choice of shade plants available, you won't be short of colours. On the contrary, it's in the early summer that the ornamental shrubs and taller perennials really come into their own. They spread out, often taking over where another plant has finished off, so that there is always something new to be found.

Planting suggestion

A stepped display with taller plants behind means you will be able to see everything properly. However, the early-flowering perennials may leave spaces, so the later-flowering *Aconitum* in the middle should cover any gaps with its tall sprays of flowers. *Aconitum* is poisonous, so if you have small children you should replace it with *Actaea* or *Anemone hupehensis*.

The perennials will spread horizontally, so they should interweave with one other along the boundaries, emphasising the character of each individual plant. This planting should be easy to maintain. The plants merge together increasingly through the seasons as the foxglove and *Thalictrum* (meadow rue) self-seed.

Fuchsia magellanica may need some protection in order to remain hardy. The above-ground shoots should die back with the frost, so that new growth can begin from the root stock in the late spring. In milder areas, the shrub should survive with no protection, but in very cold areas, if the ground remains free of snow, you can protect the rootstock from hard frosts with a mixture of compost and leaf mulch.

You could also add a few spring flowers such as winter aconite (*Eranthis hyemalis*), snowdrops (*Galanthus*) or Siberian squill (*Scilla siberica*). These will act as a kind of hors d'oeuvre without stealing the

Siberian squill (Scilla siberica) *self-seeds readily, covering large areas within a few years.*

...how from the summer beauties.

Vagabonds in the shade

Many perennials will self-seed in the garden. This will not only

enable them to spread and establish themselves, but will also give the display a certain romantic flair, with an ever-changing scene that is full of new surprises.

The following garden perennials will spread readily by self-seeding:

- *Alchemilla mollis* (lady's mantle)
- *Aquilegia vulgaris* (common columbine/granny's bonnets)
- *Arum italicum*
- *Digitalis purpurea* (foxglove)
- *Geranium phaeum* (mourning widow)

If you observe the flowers of *Phlox divaricata* at different times of day, you will discover that their blue is always changing into yet another magical shade. This popular perennial is also much sought-after for its beautiful scent.

- *Hesperis matronalis* (dame's violet/sweet rocket)
- *Lunaria annua* (honesty)
- *Scilla siberica* (Siberian squill)
- *Viola odorata* (sweet violet).

1 *Astrantia major* (masterwort)

2 *Digitalis purpurea* (foxglove)

3 *Thalictrum aquilegifolium*

4 *Aconitum carmichaelii* 'Arendsii'

5 *Fuchsia magellanica* var. *gracilis*

6 *Geranium endressii*

7 *Thalictrum delavayi* syn. *T. dipterocarpum*

8 *Stachys grandiflora*

9 *Phlox divaricata*

10 *Tiarella wherryi*

11 *Lamium maculatum* (spotted deadnettle)

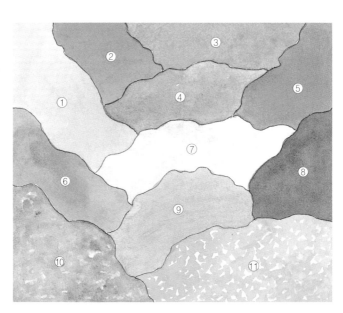

Autumn beauties

In the autumn, as the leaves begin to turn, a lot starts to happen in the shade. Late flowers combine with brightly coloured berries and glorious new leaf colours to create some beautiful sights.

A backdrop of evergreen trees or shrubs makes an excellent foil for this collection of autumn beauties. The lighter-coloured flowers will stand out well against the green (which is not liable to turn brown), while there is no danger of low-growing flowers becoming covered with dead leaves.

The poisonous orange-red berries of Arum italicum *stand out in the shade against the darker colours of the foliage.*

Planting suggestion

This autumn bed changes almost imperceptibly from summer into autumn. The Japanese anemone appears as early as the end of August,

when *Actaea simplex* (syn. *Cimicifuga simplex*) is already under starter's orders. By the time the last of the *Geranium macrorrhizum* has flowered, the tiny white stars of *Aster divaricatus* start to appear.

As the nights become colder, so the leaves begin to turn. *Hosta, Bergenia, Aruncus* and *Waldsteinia* are transformed, adding bright red and elegant bronze to the medley of colours. In between these plants, the false spikenard (*Smilacina racemosa*) displays its reddish fruits, while the tufted hair grass shows off its autumn clothing. There then

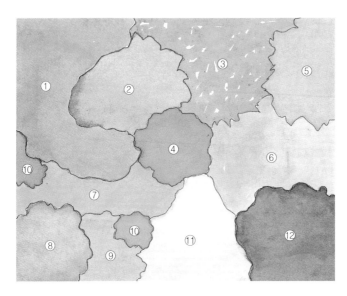

1 *Anemone hupehensis* (Japanese anemone)
2 *Hosta siedboldiana* 'Elegans'
3 *Deschampsia cespitosa* (tufted hair grass)
4 *Smilacina racemosa* (false spikena
5 *Actaea simplex* syn. *Cimicifuga simplex*
6 *Aster divaricatus*
7 *Geranium macrorrhizum* 'Spessart'
8 *Bergenia* 'Eroica'
9 *Aruncus aethusifolius* (dwarf goatsbeard)
10 *Colchicum autumnale* (autumn crocus)
11 *Waldsteinia geoides*
12 *Bergenia* 'Abendglut'

Autumn beauties

Common name / botanical name	Height (cm/in)	Flowering time / flower colour	Decorative autumn features	Notes
White baneberry (*Actaea pachypoda*)	50 (20)	May–June insignificant	white berries	*A. erythropoda* has red berries
Arum italicum	40 (16)	May yellow cob wrapped in white leaf	orange-red berries	berries poisonous
Cyclamen hederifolium	15 (6)	August–September pink	beautiful, long-lasting flowers	may self-seed
Willow gentian (*Gentiana asclepiadea*)	20–60 (8–24)	July–October dark blue	late-flowering with fresh yellow foliage	needs loamy soil; for enthusiasts
Roast beef plant (*Iris foetidissima*)	45–80 (18–32)	July pale lilac	orange-red seeds in capsules	'Variegata' has striped foliage
Liliytuft (*Liriope muscari*)	30 (12)	August–October violet	late-flowering, evergreen	in sheltered spots, flowers until first frosts
Honesty (*Lunaria annua*)	50–80 (20–32)	May–June lilac, white	seed pods covered with a silvery sheen	biennial, self-seeds readily
Bladder cherry (*Physalis alkekengi* var. *franchetii*)	45–80 (18–32)	July–September insignificant, white	large, orange-red, bladder-like fruits	can be invasive
Saxifraga fortunei	30 (12)	September–October white	gorgeous flowers	may need winter protection

follows the perfect finale as the autumn crocuses (*Colchicum autumnale*) push up through the soil to create a gorgeous splash of lilac-pink.

This display also provides some high points in the spring and summer, such as when the *Bergenia*, *Waldsteinia* and *Aruncus* come into flower, not to mention the beauty of the *Hosta* leaves or the pretty spikes on the *Deschampsia*.

Autumn crocuses are perhaps the most beautiful of all the autumn-flowering bulb plants.

Autumn crocuses (*Colchicum autumnale*) are normally planted in August, and therefore make ideal space-fillers. The double varieties produce an even more intense display of colours, though some people feel that their dense clumps of flowers look rather unnatural.

Winter evergreens

Gardens are normally quiet in the winter, but there is always something of interest to be found there, and it can be a delightful surprise to discover something new.

Evergreens are especially important in winter, and there is a wide choice of both shrubs and perennials available. These include, for example, box (*Buxus sempervirens*) and *Rhododendron* as well as periwinkle (*Vinca*) and *Bergenia* hybrids.

But winter isn't the only reason for planting evergreens, since they have plenty of other advantages. They require relatively little maintenance, for

Winter frost settles on the leaves of Pachysandra terminalis, *highlighting their edges and giving them extra definition.*

example, because they don't shed lots of leaves in the autumn.

The leaves themselves are usually hard and leathery, with a thick skin or a layer of wax to prevent water loss in winter. They therefore possess a well-defined structure that contrasts well with softer foliage.

Evergreens can also have beautiful flowers, as rhododendrons amply demonstrate with their gorgeous displays of blooms.

Planting suggestion

The planting suggested here makes an ideal design for a shady garden, or for a bed that needs to look really good all year round (it may, for example, be clearly visible from the living room).

The design mainly involves ground-cover plants that spread outwards rather than upwards. The only exceptions are the *Euphorbia* and the fern, which rise up amid a carpet of green. Their contrasting structure helps to enliven the display, which is reminiscent of a large rug made up of lots of different strands of wool.

As winter retreats, so the plants start to flower. The first

changes become visible in the elaborately named *Euphorbia amygdaloides* var. *robbiae*. First the ends of the shoots turn over to look like walking-stick handles, then they stand up like bunches of feathers. The yellowish-green flowers appear amid regular rows of leaves along the stem.

The lesser periwinkle (*Vinca minor*) produces tiny blue flowers in the shape of stars, while the *Waldsteinia ternata* forms small yellow buds that swell up as they emerge through the leaves. The gorgeous flowers of the *Euphorbia pinatum colchicum* seem almost to dance, while the *Pachysandra* is similarly generous with its blooms.

One effect of all these colour is that you scarcely notice that the hard fern (*Blechnum spicant*) is beginning to fade. Fresh new fronds soon appear however, from the very heart of the plant.

After the *Euphorbia amygdaloides* has finished flowering, it should be drastically cut back. Summer pruning should leave only five or six young shoots. These will quickly sprout and develop into small bushes that might otherwise become weak and fall apart.

Vinca minor (lesser periwinkle)

Pachysandra terminalis

Asarum europaeum (wild ginger)

Euphorbia amygdaloides var. robbiae

Waldsteinia ternata

Euphorbia pinnatum colchicum

Blechnum spicant (hard fern)

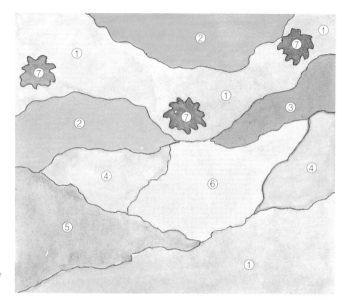

Don't forget the ivy

If you want to have evergreens in your garden, you should always consider using ivy (Hedera), which comes in many different forms with variegated or otherwise interestingly patterned leaves.
There are all sorts of things that can be done with ivy. You could, for example, simply allow the shoots to spread across the ground. Or you could train them up a wall, creating a visual link between the wall and the plants growing in front of it. Another interesting option might be to train the ivy around wire figures or shapes such as balls, rabbits or even bears.

Woody evergreens that can be cut to shape, such as box or yew, create interest throughout the year while always remaining in the background.

A spherical box tree in a tub makes the ideal space filler, and can always be placed in a gap to create a point of interest in places where winter plants have become all too monotonous.

Flowers all year round

Perhaps everyone's ideal would be to have a flower bed with blooms throughout the year, but this is not easy to achieve. Firstly, the plants shouldn't simply flower one after each other in a row. It's better to achieve a dynamic network of plants with overlapping flowering seasons. Winter will still be a rather bare season, even with a large selection of plants. But if you want flowers in a bed from early spring right through to late autumn, there are ways of achieving this.

Campanula portenschlagiana *is easy to look after and produces carpets of long-lasting violet-coloured flowers.*

The important thing is to include lots of different plants with flowering seasons that overlap.

Planting suggestion

The gardening year starts with bang as the Japanese azaleas come into flower. Their strikin blooms have a magic attractior all of their own, though it mig be a good idea to plant a few snowdrops in any gaps in the surrounding beds, if only to keep them company. Azalea bushes don't grow very tall, ar the flowers may be so densely packed that not a single leaf is visible beneath them.

Soon afterwards the *Deschampsia* begins to sprout while the goatsbeard (*Aruncus dioicus*) unfurls its fresh-greer

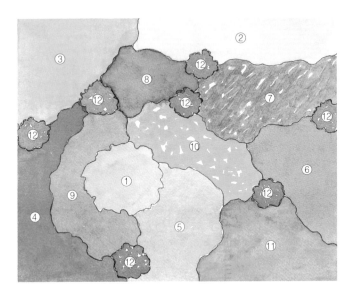

1 *Rhododendron* Japonicum hybrid (Japanese [evergreen] azalea)

2 *Clematis × jouiniana*

3 *Aruncus dioicus* (goatsbeard)

4 *Anemone hupehensis* (Japanese anemone)

5 *Campanula portenschlagiana*

6 *Chelone obliqua* (turtlehead)

7 *Deschampsia cespitosa* (tufted hai grass)

8 *Astilbe* 'Straussenfeder'

9 *Hesperis matrionalis* (dame's violet/sweet rocket)

10 *Polemonium reptans* (Jacob's lado

11 *Geranium × magnificum*

12 *Aquilegia vulgaris* (granny's bonne

symphony in yellow – tall sprays of Lysimachia punctata *and yellow clouds of dy's mantle* (Alchemilla mollis).

aves and pushes up long, athery sprays of flowers. You should try to train the roots of the *Campanula ortenschlagiana* so that they over the azaleas during the ummer. When autumn comes ou'll need to cut back these roots to allow the bushes to recover.

Soon the bed is so thickly rrewn with loose sprays of *quilegia* that the whole bed eems to be in flower. In the reantime, *Geranium* and *esperis* (dame's violet/sweet ocket) are preparing for their ntry, while *Campanula* and *olemonium* are equally impa-ent. These last two perennials o well in light or even dappled shade, but should not be kept in too dark a position.

Campanula and *Geranium* × *magnificum* provide colour for many weeks, whereas the *Hesperis* soon finishes flower-ing, allowing the Japanese anemone to step into the gaps left behind.

As the *Deschampsia* begins to fade with the high summer, so the *Clematis* × *jouiniana* comes into full bloom. This particular hybrid has a gorgeous scent. It doesn't climb very much, preferring instead to drape itself around the surroun-ding perennials. Its flowers will last until October.

In high summer the goats-beard is replaced by *Astilbe*, whose gently drooping salmon-pink blooms provide colour well into the autumn. The pink is then augmented by the colours of turtlehead and Japanese anemone. All three plants vie for attention in an Indian summer that with luck may last until early November.

Long-flowering shade plants

Some shade plants will flower for a very long time, including the following:

- giant bellflower (*Campanula latifolia*)
- foxglove (*Digitalis*)
- *Fuchsia magellanica* var. *gracilis*
- plantain lily (*Hosta*)
- deadnettle (*Lamium*)
- Welsh poppy (*Meconopsis cambrica*)
- flowering tobacco (*Nicotiana sylvestris*)
- Jacob's ladder (*Polemonium caeruleum*)

An easy-care planting

Gardeners are often reluctant to plant anything in the shade simply on the basis that 'It's not much use without any sun.' Yet it is just as important to plant in the shade as anywhere else, and not just with bushes and shrubs but with ground-cover plants. If you don't, the weeds will soon arrive to fill the space, and before long they will start to proliferate. So if you have to take the time to plant something here anyway, you might just as well take the trouble to plant something that looks really good.

On the other hand, it's quite understandable if you want to expend the minimum of energy here and concentrate on sunnier parts of the garden. The best way to achieve this is to use strong plants that spread vigorously.

In the early spring, periwinkle and *Pachysandra terminalis* can be cut back using a lawn mower with the blades set high. This doesn't require much effort, and is only necessary if the plants start to look bare.

A few rays of sunshine penetrate the barely open fronds of ostrich ferns (Matteuccia struthiopteris) *amid hosts of creamy-white comfrey flowers.*

Planting suggestion

This suggested planting combines four different ground-cover plants that intermingle with each other. The comfrey (*Symphytum*) and the lesser periwinkle (*Vinca minor*) cover the bed with blue and violet flowers during the spring. In the summer these plants are replaced by the white flowers of *Pachysandra terminalis* and the raspberry-pink blooms of *Geranium macrorrhizum*, which later on provides bright autumn tints. This plant also has strongly aromatic leaves that keep dogs and cats away, so it's a good idea to plant it along the front edge of the garden or garden bed.

Planting the taller fringecup (*Tellima grandiflora*) at the back adds some further interest to the display. The boundaries between the ground-cover plants can be filled with snowdrops (*Galanthus*) and bluebells (*Hyacinthoides*) to provide extra interest in the spring. And finally, a large tub full of *Campanula poscharskyana* will add yet more colour during th

ummer months, especially if
he tub is painted in bright
olours.
Instead of the tub of *Campan-
la*, you could place some
rightly coloured object that
reates a further contrasting
imension.

Tellima grandiflora (fringecups)

Hyacinthoides hispanica (Spanish bluebell)

Pachysandra terminalis

Symphytum grandiflorum (Turkish comfrey)

Geranium macrorrhizum 'Ingwersen's Variety'

Vinca minor (lesser periwinkle)

*Tellima grandiflora (fringecups)
produces veils of flowers above dense
clumps of foliage – a robust plant
requiring a minimum of maintenance.*

7 *Galanthus nivalis* (common snowdrop)

8 *Campanula poscharskyana* in a tub

Plants for damp situations

Damp areas along the banks of
a stream or a pond are special
situations that not every garden
possesses. Such areas should
not be ignored, as they provide
a habitat for a wonderful range
of plants.

Ponds and streams are particularly attractive features to have
in a garden. The sound of the
water has a calming effect, and
water-loving animals such as
frogs can enrich any garden.

It's important, however, to
distinguish between dry and
wet riverbanks. The amount of
moisture available will depend,
for example, on how a pond
has been built.

If you have any problems with slugs
and snails, then you should be
careful when planting on riverbanks.
Wet ground provides the ideal
conditions for these greedy little
pests. The best solution is to plant
rough grasses or *Astilbe*, which
cause problems for such soft-
bodied creatures. Lady's mantle
(*Alchemilla mollis*) also has coarse
leaves that slugs don't really like.

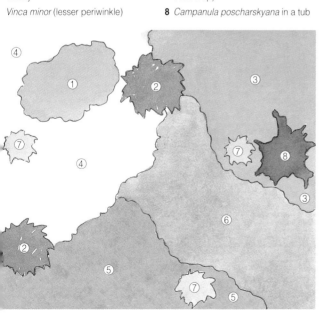

Plants for damp shade				
Common name / botanical name	Height (cm/in)	Flowering time / flower colour	Foliage	Notes
Lady's mantle (*Alchemilla mollis*)	40 (16)	June–August / greenish yellow	dull green	decorative foliage
***Astilbe* species and** varieties	25–120 (10–48)	June–October / pink, red, white	dark green	flowers give visual interest, plants resistant to slugs
Cardamine trifolia	15 (6)	April–May / white	dark green, shiny	develops dense carpet of foliage
Umbrella plant (*Darmera peltata* syn. *Peltiphyllum peltatum*)	80 (32)	April–May / pinkish white	shield-like, long stems	gorgeous autumn colouring
Meadowsweet (*Filipendula ulmaria*)	70 (28)	July–August / creamy white	fresh green, finely divided	'Plena' has double flowers
Lythrum virgatum	80 (32)	July–September / salmon-pink	mid-green	attracts butterflies
Welsh poppy (*Meconopsis cambrica*)	30 (12)	June–September / yellow	light green	self-seeds
Sensitive fern (*Onoclea sensibilis*)	45 (18)		light green, compound pinnate	pale-red creepers
Royal fern (*Osmunda regalis*)	100 (40)		light green, compound pinnate	prefers acid soils
Primula viallii	30 (12)	June–July / violet-red	fresh green	may need winter protection in cold areas
***Tradescantia* hybrids**	50 (20)	June–August / blue, white, carmine	grass-like	strong, decorative foliage

Planting suggestion

This planting is intended for a wet riverbank, as the plants chosen prefer damp or wet ground and should never be allowed to become dry. The plants are stepped up gradually from the water's edge. This means you need a seat on the opposite bank, or a narrow path along the bank, so that you can enjoy the beauty of these plants to the full.

The planting has been designed to provide flowers for

The gold-coloured blooms of the globeflower (Trollius europaeus) can add to the beauty of a river bank.

the maximum period – hence the particular combination of *Primula* species that includes both spring- and summer-flowering species (*P. veris* and *P. florindae*).

The other plants carry on much the same dialogue, with spring-flowering leopard's bar (*Doronicum orientale*) and globeflower (*Trollius europaeus*) opposed to summer-flowering *Geum coccineum* an creeping Jenny (*Lysimachia nummularia*).

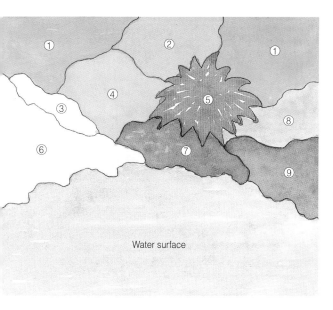

Water surface

1 *Ligularia dentata* 'Othello'
2 *Aruncus dioicus* 'Zweiweltenkind' (goatsbeard)
3 *Kirengeshoma palmata*
4 *Doronicum orientale* (leopard's bane)
5 *Carex pendula* (pendulous sedge)
6 *Lysimachia nummularia* (creeping Jenny)
7 *Primula veris* (cowslip) and *P. florindae* (giant cowslip)
8 *Trollius europaeus* (globeflower)
9 *Geum coccineum*

In the early summer, the goatsbeard (*Aruncus dioicus* 'Zweiweltenkind') and pendulous sedge (*Carex pendula*) create a fresh-green backdrop with natural-looking flowers – a role assumed in high summer by the *Ligularia dentata*.

The autumn months are then dominated by the stately presence of the *Kirengeshoma palmata*.

The umbrella plant (Darmera peltata) *develops strong leaves on long stems that appear after the flowers in spring. It forms thick clumps around a pond.*

at a glance

- There are lots of shrubs, perennials and bulb plants available for shady gardens.

- A single theme gives a certain unity to a display, and may involve the flower colours, the foliage or the different growth habits.

- You could design shade plants to create an all-year-round display, or alternatively you could concentrate on plants that flower in one season only, simply providing other attractions for the rest of the year.

- Shady gardens have their equivalents in the wild, which provide picturesque models for natural-looking spring displays or riverbank plantings.

The best shade plants

There is no end to the number of different shrubs, perennials and bulb plants that will thrive in the shade and at the same time make for interesting plantings. Many tried-and-tested species and varieties are described below together with their uses and requirements.

This chapter contains brief descriptions of the most important shade plants, including both species and varieties. They have been divided into five sections:

- herbaceous perennials
- grasses
- ferns
- bulb plants
- shrubs.

The use of botanical names

The common names for plants vary enormously, often according to region, and for this reason they can sometimes be misleading. Botanical names, which are mostly Latin in origin, are specifically designed to avoid such misunderstandings.

Each botanical name is given in italics and consists of the **generic name** (genus) followed by the **specific name**

◄ The wood anemone, which forms a thick carpet of flowers below trees, is a sure harbinger of spring.

(species); the latter usually describes specific characteristics. A name (not in italics) that follows this in inverted commas is the **variety name**, which describes a form with particular characteristics.

The descriptions in each section of this chapter are given in alphabetic order of botanical names. The information on growth height and flowering seasons (see yellow panel) gives average figures, and both factors may vary according to local conditions.

Herbaceous perennials

Herbaceous (i.e. non-woody) perennials are the most important plants for shady gardens. Those with decorative flowers or foliage are particularly interesting from a gardening point of view. Ground-cover plants make for easy-care plantings, and can be nicely offset by taller perennials as well as grasses, ferns and bulb plants.

Use of symbols

The symbols provide brief information about the flowering period and the growth height of each plant:

Flowering period

🌣 4–7   The months when the plant is in flower (here April to July).

Growth height

↑ 20–30   Average growth
(8–12)   height in cm (in) for varieties as well as species.

Monkshood
***Aconitum* species and varieties**

🌣 7–10   ↑ 80–200 (30–80)

Flowers: blue, rarely yellow, pink or white, helmet-shaped, in loose or dense spikes.

Foliage: shiny-green, deeply divided into three to five parts.

Growth habit: upright, clump-forming.

Position: cool, damp, nutrient-rich soils.

Good companions: *Geranium*, *Astilbe*, Japanese anemones.

Mookshood (Aconitum)

Notes: *A. carmichaelii* 'Arendsii' grows up to 120 cm (48 in) tall and produces azure flowers from September to October. The 100-cm (40-in) tall flowers of the common monkshood (*A. napellus*) are deep blue and appear in July. *A. × cammarum* produces bluish-white flowers on 150-cm (60-in) stems. Wolfsbane (*A. lycoctonum*), on the other hand, has pale-yellow flowers, which make a popular change from the usual blue.

Bugle
Ajuga reptans

✿ 5–6 ⬆ 10–15 (4–6)

Flowers: blue, white or pink, lipped, in dense spikes.

Foliage: oval with stems, in rosettes.

Growth habit: spreads horizontally by means of runners.

Position: damp, nutrient-rich soils.

Good companions: *Aconitum, Waldsteinia, Deschampsia, Dryopteris.*

Notes: *A. reptans* 'Atropurpurea' has brownish-red leaves and blue flowers; 'Riesmöwe' has white flowers and light-green leaves. See photo on page 82.

Japanese anemones
Anemone hupehensis, Anemone × hybrida

✿ 8–9 ⬆ 50–100 (20–40)

Flowers: pink or white cup-shaped flowers 5–6 cm (2 in) across, in loose sprays; may be double.

Foliage: dull green, tripartite, with irregularly toothed edges.

Growth habit: bushy, spreads slowly by means of rhizomes.

Position: loose, humus-rich soils.

Good companions: *Aconitun Actaea, Matteuccia, Rhodo-dendron.*

Wood anemone
Anemone nemorosa

✿ 3–4 ⬆ 15–20 (6–8)

Flowers: white cups on tall stems, closed at night or in du weather.

Foliage: dark-green, tripartite, deeply divided leaves with sho stems.

Growth habit: carpet-forming spreads by rhizomes.

Position: damp, humus-rich soils.

Good companions: *Vinca, Pulmonaria, Corydalis, Viola odorata.*

Anemone × hybrida

Common columbine (Aquilegia vulgaris) *is also known as granny's bonnets.*

Common columbine, granny's bonnets
Aquilegia vulgaris

✿ 5–6 ❚ 40–80 (16–32)

Flowers: blue, violet, white or pink, spurred.

Foliage: blue-green, tripartite structure.

Growth habit: upright, branch-ing stems.

Position: humus-rich soils.

Good companions: *Dicentra, Geranium, Waldsteinia, Luzula, Hakonechloa macra.*

Notes: self-seeds readily and spreads quickly.

Arum italicum

✿ 4–5 ❚ 20–30 (8–12)

Flowers: yellowish spadix in white sheath with red spots.

Foliage: strikingly dark-green, arrow-shaped leaves with silvery veins.

Growth habit: loose clumps.

Position: prefers damp soils; plants die back after flowering and are therefore drought-tolerant.

Good companions: *Astilbe, Aquilegia, Carex plantaginea, Lonicera,* ferns.

Notes: *Arum* species are sometimes sold as tubers. The striking red berries appear in the autumn (see photo on page 26).

Goatsbeard
Aruncus dioicus

✿ 6–7 ❚ 150–200 (60–80)

Flowers: white to creamy, on tall, branching sprays.

Foliage: fresh green, large, pinnate, toothed.

Growth habit: clump-forming.

Position: damp loam, rich in humus and nutrients.

Good companions: *Aconitum, Campanula, Geranium, Deschampsia.*

Notes: good specimen plant; the variety known as *A. dioicus* 'Zweiweltenkind' has creamy-white flowers and grows up to 150 cm (5 ft) tall.

Astilbe species and varieties

✿ 6–10 ❚ 15–150 (6–60)

Flowers: white, pink, violet and various reds, appearing on feathery sprays.

Foliage: dark green, pinnate.

Growth habit: clump-forming; *A. chinensis* var. *pumila* spreads by runners.

Position: humus-rich soils.

Good companions: *Actaea, Bergenia, Hosta,* Japanese anemones, hart's-tongue fern.

Goatsbeard (Aruncus dioicus)

Astilbe *in white and red*

Notes: there are many different kinds of *Astilbe*:

- *A. arendsii* hybrids: flowers July to September, compact sprays; low- and medium-growing varieties; height 50–70 cm (20–28 in).

- *A. chinensis* var. *pumila*: flowers August to October, lilac-pink sprays; height 20 cm (8 in); ideal for ground cover.

- *A. japonica* hybrids: flowers late June to July, pyramidal sprays; height 50–60 cm (20–24 in).

- *A. simplicifolia* hybrids: flowers late July to August, overhanging pyramidal sprays; height 40–60 cm (16–24 in).

- *A. thunbergii* hybrids: flowers July to August, loosely branching, on overhanging sprays; height 80–120 cm (32–48 in).

Wild ginger
Asarum europaeum

 3–4   5–15 (2–6)

Flowers: insignificant, brown, bell-shaped, short stems on the ground.

Foliage: ovate, shiny green, scented, evergreen.

Growth habit: creeping, spreads slowly.

Position: humus-rich soils.

Good companions: *Omphalodes verna*, *Hepatica*, *Primula*, *Vinca*, *Cyclamen*.

Notes: the rhizomes spread on top of the soil, so don't plant too deep, and don't hoe between plants.

Masterwort
Astrantia major

6–7   30–90 (12–35)

Flowers: white to pink, stemmed, button-like umbels i star-shaped sheaths.

Foliage: lobed or divided into five parts.

Growth habit: clump-forming.

Position: nutrient-rich soils.

Good companions: *Brunnera Campanula*, *Dryopteris*, hart's tongue fern.

Masterwort (Astrantia major)

runnera macrophylla is sometimes nown as Slberian bugloss.

ergenia **hybrids**

❀ 3–5 (some varieties will ower again later)

⬆ 25–60 (10–24)

lowers: white, pink and red, ell-shaped, carried in umbels n strong stems.

oliage: large, leathery, mostly vergreen, often with striking utumn colours.

Growth habit: large, vigorous lumps.

Position: normal garden soils.

Good companions: *Astilbe, Waldsteinia, Geranium, Aconitum, Hakonechloa macra*, royal fern.

Notes: lots of varieties (see also photo on page 93).

Brunnera macrophylla

❀ 4–5 ⬆ 40–60 (16–24)

Flowers: sky-blue, similar to forget-me-nots, borne in loose umbels.

Foliage: fresh green, heart-shaped with stems, rough.

Growth habit: clump-forming.

Position: humus-rich soils.

Good companions: *Epimedium, Narcissus, Primula, Deschampsia*, lady fern.

Notes: 'Langtrees' is a particularly interesting variety with silvery-spotted foliage.

Giant bellflower *Campanula latifolia*

❀ 6–7 ⬆ 80–100 (32–40)

Flowers: violet-blue, pointed, in loose racemes with leaves up to the tips.

Foliage: main leaves large and heart-shaped, stem leaves small and elongated.

Growth habit: upright, clump-forming.

Position: dampish, humus-rich soils.

Good companions: *Actaea, Aruncus, Deschampsia, Luzula, Pachysandra*.

Notes: *C. latifolia* var. *macrantha* has even larger, darker-coloured flowers. *C. latifolia* var. *alba* is the same with white flowers.

Actaea syn. *Cimicifuga* species

❀ 7–10 ⬆ 60–220 (24–100)

Flowers: thin racemes of small, white flowers.

Foliage: dark green, pinnate.

Giant bellflower (Campanula latifolia)

Growth habit: clump-forming.

Position: humus-rich soils.

Good companions: *Aconitum*, *Campanula latifolia*, Japanese anemones, *Astilbe*, *Rhododendron*.

Notes: *A. cordifolia* (syn. *C. cordifolia*) has narrow, upright racemes of yellowish-white flowers from mid-August, and grows to over 200 cm (80 in).

A. simplex (syn. *C. simplex*) has dense, overhanging racemes of white flowers in September and October, and grows up to 140 cm (56 in) tall.

A. racemosa (syn. *C. racemosa*) produces 40-cm (16-in) long racemes of fragrant creamy-white flowers in September, and grows to 200 cm (80 in).

Clematis species

❀ 5–9 ↕ 40–300 (16–120)

Flowers: blue to violet, white and red; single flowers bell-shaped; otherwise in racemes.

Fruits: feathery seed heads.

Foliage: dark green, tripartite.

Growth habit: clump-forming, creeping or climbing.

Position: soils rich in humus and nutrients.

Good companions: *Aconitum*, *Geranium, Hakonechloa macra, Heuchera, Kirengeshoma palmata, Rhododendron*, yew.

Notes: unlike other well-known climbers, *Clematis* includes several non-woody species.

Clematis × jouiniana

C. heracleifolia produces light blue, hyacinth-like flowers that grow in handfuls among the upper leaf axils. It has an upright habit, growing to 100 cm (40 in).

C. integrifolia forms clumps and grows to 60 cm (24 in). The bell-shaped indigo-blue flowers appear singly from June to September.

C. × jouiniana is a partial climber that grows to 200 cm (80 in) and creates a good mulch layer for spring flowers. In August the whole plant is covered with upright sprays of light-blue flowers.

Actaea simplex *syn.* Cimicifuga simplex

Bleeding heart (Dicentra spectabilis)

ily-of-the-valley
onvallaria majalis

❀ 5   ⬆ 15–25 (6–10)

lowers: bell-shaped fragrant /hite flowers in erect racemes.

oliage: fresh green, broadly vate.

|rowth habit: spreads by 1eans of underground reepers.

'osition: humus-rich soils nder trees and shrubs.

|ood companions: *Aquilegia, /osta, Omphalodes verna, /inca, Carex*, sensitive fern, *Dryopteris*.

|otes: see photo on page 10.

Corydalis species

❀ 3–9   ⬆ 10–50 (4–20)

lowers: yellow, pink, white, .lue, with long spurs, in acemes on stems.

Corydalis

Foliage: fresh green, pinnate, very soft.

Growth habit: bushy, branched.

Position: humus-rich soils.

Good companions: *Hosta, Polemonium, Carex*, royal fern, *Polystichum*.

Notes: propagates by seed, which is spread by ants.

- *C. cava*: up to 35 cm (14 in), produces dense white or magenta racemes.
- *C. cheilanthifolia*: brownish-green, frond-like leaves, yellow flowers May–June.
- *C. flexuosa*: height 20–30 cm (8–12 in), flowers from April to June, different varieties.

Dicentra species and varieties

❀ 4–9   ⬆ 20–80 (8–32)

Flowers: white, pink, heart-shaped, in racemes on stems.

Foliage: blue-green, pinnate, soft.

Growth habit: bushy, spread-ing clumps.

Position: garden soils rich in humus and nutrients.

Good companions: *Aquilegia, Campanula latifolia, Primula, Geranium*, ferns.

Notes: *D. eximia* produces heart-shaped pink flowers from May to September, growing in racemes among fern-like leaves.

D. *formosa* grows to 30 cm (12 in), with pink flowers above the finely divided leaves.

The pink-and-white flowers of D. *spectabilis* (bleeding heart) – a classic cottage-garden plant – hang in rows on 80-cm (32-in) stems. D. *spectabilis* 'Alba' has pure-white flowers.

Epimedium *makes a good ground-cover plant.*

Foxglove
Digitalis purpurea

 6–7 100–140 (40–56)

Flowers: white or light- to dark-pink bells on candle-shaped racemes.

Foliage: large, rough, pointed ovate.

Growth habit: upright, rosette-like, usually biennial.

Position: humus-rich, slightly acid soils.

Good companions: *Aruncus, Brunnera, Campanula, Deschampsia, Rhododendron.*

Notes: D. × *mertonensis* bears large, salmon-pink flowers and grows to 80–100 cm (32–40 in). D. *ferruginea* only grows to 60 cm (24 in) in height and develops light-yellow flowers with red-brown markings. Both species flower at the same time as the foxglove. See also photo on page 86.

Epimedium species and varieties

 4–5 15–35 (6–14)

Flowers: small, white, yellow, lilac or pink, with several sprays on each stem.

Foliage: dark green, sometimes bronze, in three or five parts, sometimes evergreen.

Growth habit: cushion- or carpet-forming ground-cover plant; spreads by runners.

Position: damp, humus-rich soils.

Good companions: *Hosta, Tiarella, Waldsteinia,* low-growing *Carex.*

Notes: E. *grandiflorum* develops large, deep-pink flowers and grows to 25 cm (10 in). The evergreen E. *pinnatum,* now known as *Euphorbia pinnatum,* has yellow flowers and grows to 30 cm (12 in); its subspecies E. *pinnatum colchicum* make excellent evergreen ground cover. The yellow-flowered *Epimedium* × *versicolor* grow vigorously to 35 cm (14 in). E. × *youngianum* grows slowly into 20-cm (8-in) high cushion with lilac-pink flowers. E. × *youngianum* 'Niveum' has showy white flowers.

Epimedium *flowers*

Euphorbia griffithii

Euphorbia amygdaloides var. robbiae (syn. *E. robbiae*)

❀ 4–7 ⬆ 50–60 (20–24)

Flowers: yellowish-green, in umbels.

Foliage: bright green, blunt, elongated, reddish autumn tints.

Growth habit: clump-forming.

Position: well-drained soils.

Good companions: *Hosta, Brunnera, Helleborus,* ferns.

Notes: *E. griffithii* has red-leaved varieties that light up semi-shaded places with their orange-red bracts. Of these, 'Dixter' and 'Fireglow' produce deep-red colours and grow to 80–100 cm (32–40 in).

Lady's eardrops *Fuchsia magellanica varieties*

❀ 6–10 ⬆ 100–180 (40–70)

Flowers: red, white and violet, hanging on long stems.

Foliage: dark green, small, lanceolate, short stems.

Growth habit: upright shrub, usually regrowing from base if top growth is killed in winter.

Position: soils rich in humus and nutrients; crown may need protection in cold areas.

Good companions: *Aconitum, Actaea, Hosta,* Japanese anemones, *Thalictrum.*

Notes: usually needs to be cut back to the ground in early spring. Other hardy fuchsias that can be treated similarly include: *F. magellanica* var. *gracilis* (pretty red-and-blue flowers; up to 80 cm/32 in);

F. 'Mme Cornelissen' (red-and-white flowers; up to 120 cm/48 in); *F.* 'Riccartonii' (red-and-violet flowers; up to 140 cm/56 in). See photo on page 24.

Sweet woodruff *Galium odoratum*

❀ 4–5 ⬆ 10–20 (4–8)

Flowers: white, loosely branching umbels, scented.

Foliage: lanceolate, in tight whorls.

Growth habit: spreading.

Position: humus-rich garden soils.

Good companions: *Anemone nemorosa, Asarum, Hepatica, Primula, Geranium.*

Sweet woodruff (Galium odoratum)

Wood cranesbill (Geranium sylvaticum)

Cranesbill
***Geranium* species and varieties**

❀ 5–8   ⬆ 25–60 (10–24)

Flowers: pink, violet, blue, saucer- to cup-shaped.

Foliage: fan-like in structure, lobed or divided.

Growth habit: bushy or cushion-forming, usually spreading.

Position: normal garden soils.

Good companions: *Astilbe*, *Cyclamen*, *Dicentra*, *Galium odoratum*, *Hosta*, royal fern.

Notes: the foliage may be as decorative as the flowers. The following species are good for half-shade on the edge of woodland:

• *G. endressii* – vigorous, fresh-pink flowers from May to August, tolerates pressure from roots. Good variety: 'Wargrave Pink', with small,

Geranium macrorrhizum

salmon-pink flowers; *G.* × *oxonianum* 'Rose Clair' is very similar, having deep-p[ ] flowers with white veins.

• *G. himalayense* – dense carpet of foliage with good autumn colouring; violet-b[ ] flowers from June to July.

• *G. nodosum* – good for dee[ ] shade; lilac-pink flowers las[t]-ing for a long period (May [ ] August).

• *G. macrorrhizum* – creepin[g] ground-cover plant with aromatic leaves, bearing pi[n] or pinkish-white flowers fr[ ] May to July; striking autumn[ ] colouring; shouldn't be use[d] over too wide an area.

• wood cranesbill (*G. sylvati-cum*) – violet flowers from June to July. Interesting varieties: 'Album' (white), 'Mayflower' (light blue).

Hellebore
***Helleborus* species and varieties**

❀ 12–5   ⬆ 20–60 (8–24)

Flowers: white, red or green bells or cups, with large stamens.

Foliage: dark green, leathery, palmate, sometimes toothed, long stems, evergreen.

Growth habit: clump-forming.

Position: lime- and humus-rich soils, loose, well-drained and preferably dry.

Good companions: *Brunnera, Cyclamen, Primula, Pulmonaria,* evergreen ferns.

Notes: long-lived plants, developing into large clumps over the years by means of shallow rhizomes. The most important garden species include:

* Christmas rose (*H. niger*) – large white flowers may open as early as December; grows to 20–30 cm (8–12 in).
* Lenten rose (*H. orientalis*) – grows up to 50 cm (20 in) tall; many varieties with red,

Lenten rose (Helleborus orientalis)

pink or white flowers, some double or beautifully spotted in the middle.

* stinking hellebore (*H. foetidus*) – bushy, evergreen, growing up to 50 cm (20 in) in height and bearing bell-shaped green flowers in late winter.

Hepatica species and varieties

 3–4   5–15 (2–6)

Flowers: blue, white or pink, soft cups, with large yellow stamens.

Foliage: fresh, shiny green, three- to five-lobed.

Growth habit: clump-forming, spreading.

Position: soils rich in humus and lime.

Good companions: *Anemone nemorosa, Corydalis, Helleborus, Omphalodes verna,* primrose, violet.

Notes: *H. nobilis* is evergreen in sheltered locations. There are several varieties, with flower colours varying from light to dark blue and violet.

H. transsilvanica grows into very pretty little cushions, and tolerates pressure from tree roots.

Alum root (Heuchera)

Alum root
Heuchera species and varieties

5–7   40–70 (16–28)

Flowers: sprays of white, pink or red bells on long, stiff, leafless stems.

Foliage: heart-shaped with long stems, in rosettes, evergreen.

Growth habit: bushy, clump-forming.

Position: soils rich in humus and nutrients.

Good companions: *Aquilegia*, *Arum*, *Astilbe*, *Erythronium*.

Notes: *H.* × *brizoides* includes the majority of the most important garden varieties, of which there are many. *H. micrantha* 'Palace Purple' is noted for its decorative foliage, with very large, burgundy-coloured leaves and soft-pink flowers. *H. cylindrica* 'Greenfinch' bears pale-green flowers and forms thick clumps of dark-green leaves.

Hosta sieboldiana *var.* elegans

Plantain lily, funkia
***Hosta* species and varieties**

✿ 6–10 ⬆ 20–90 (8–35)

Flowers: dense racemes of be shaped, nodding, white to da lilac flowers.

Foliage: large, heart-shaped (lanceolate, with noticeable ve structure and smooth or wavy edges; green, steel-blue, yello or white-variegated, or silvery spotted.

Good species and varieties of *Hosta*

Species or variety	Height (cm/in)	Flowering time	Flower colour	Foliage
H. fortunei var. aurea	40–50 (16–20)	July to August	violet	young leaves are bright golden-yellow; from mid-June they become light green with silvery spots; heart-shaped, medium-sized
H. 'Gold Standard'	70–80 (28–32)	July to August	lavender	yellowish green with bluish spots, deep green along margins, heart-shaped
H. lancifolia	20–40 (8–16)	August to September	dark violet	long, narrow stems with purple spots, brownish purple towards ground, leaves green, shiny on both sides, lanceolate
H. plantaginea 'Royal Standard'	50–70 (20–28)	August to September	white, fragrant	green, on long stems, large and broadly heart-shaped, slightly pointed, shiny on both sides, very elegant
H. sieboldiana var. elegans	70–90 (28–35)	July to August	white to pale violet	strong grey-blue tints, broadly heart-shaped, slightly pointed, wrinkled between the veins
Hosta 'Halcyon'	40–60 (16–24)	July to September	pale violet	broad, strong blue tints, thick-set
Hosta undulata var. univittata	25–40 (10–160)	August to September	pale violet	broadly ovate, slightly wavy, white along central rib, with narrow white stripes, leaf tip often turned to the side, appears at the end of April

Hosta comes in all sorts of colours and patterns.

Growth habit: clump-forming.
Position: soils rich in humus
and nutrients.
Good companions: *Aquilegia,
Geranium,* grasses, ferns.
Notes: growth begins relatively
late in April or May, so plants
remain bare in early spring.
There are many varieties of
Hosta, which are often classi-
fied in groups. Slugs are particularly fond of these plants,
although some varieties are less
vulnerable than others. The
best species and varieties are
given in the table opposite.

Kirengeshoma palmata

✿ 8–9 ⬆ 50–80 (20–32)

Flowers: lemon-yellow, waxy,
nodding, on overhanging
racemes.

Foliage: dull green, heart-
shaped, palmate.

Growth habit: grows vigorously into dense clumps.

Position: soils rich in humus
and nutrients.

Good companions: *Aconitum,
Actaea simplex,* Japanese
anemones, *Carex, Hosta,
Rodgersia, Matteuccia.*

Yellow archangel
Lamium galeobdolon (syn.
Lamiastrum galeobdolon)

✿ 4–7 ⬆ 20–30 (8–12)

Flowers: yellow, lipped with
helmet-shaped upper lip, never
very many.

Foliage: white-variegated, semi-
evergreen.

Growth habit: spreading,
invasive.

Position: humus-rich soils.

Good companions: *Astilbe,
Deschampsia, Geranium,
Pulmonaria,* lady fern.

Notes: vigorous ground-cover
plant that not only drives out
weeds but also any weaker-
growing perennials.

Kirengeshoma palmata

Spotted deadnettle
Lamium maculatum

 5–7   15–25 (6–10)

Flowers: reddish purple, pink or white, lipped with helmet-shaped upper lip.

Foliage: dark green, often with silvery markings.

Growth habit: creeping, spreading.

Position: humus-rich or sandy soils.

Good companions: *Geranium, Deschampsia, Leucojum, Polypodium, Pulmonaria.*

Notes: varieties with speckled or variegated foliage are especially recommended.

Spotted deadnettle

Examples of these include: 'Album' (white flowers and silvery foliage); 'Chequers' (pink flowers and silvery leaves with green edges); 'Aureum' (pale-violet flowers and yellow-and-green foliage).

Ligularia species and varieties

7–9   100–190 (40–75)

Flowers: yellow or orange, in large, radiating flower heads, spherical or umbrella-shaped sprays, or thin spikes.

Foliage: fresh green to brownish green.

Growth habit: upright, clump-forming.

Position: nutrient-rich soils.

Good companions: *Aconitum, Hosta,* Japanese anemones, *Astilbe,* royal fern.

Notes: *Ligularia* needs space to spread out on all sides.

L. dentata has large, heart-shaped leaves that are extremely decorative. In August and September this plant develops umbrella-shaped sprays of large, orange flowers at 150 cm (60 in), clear of the foliage. The variety *L. dentata* 'Desdemona' has striking brownish to purple foliage, bears reddish-orange

Ligularia przewalskii

flowers and grows up to 100 c (40 in), but is unfortunately vulnerable to slugs.

L. × *hessii* produces cob-shaped sprays of golden flowe from July to August, growing t a height of 190 cm (75 in).

L. przewalskii grows to a heig of 150 cm (60 in). It has deepl divided leaves, and produces narrow, upright spikes of yellow flowers from July to August.

Welsh poppy (Meconopsis cambrica)

oosestrife
ysimachia species and
arieties

❀ 5–8   ⬆ 5–80 (2–32)

lowers: yellow, single in *L. ummularia* (creeping Jenny), ut otherwise in racemes, mbels or spikes.

oliage: dull green, broadly nceolate to ovate.

rowth habit: creeping (*L. ummularia*) or in upright lumps.

osition: damp, nutrient-rich oils.

ood companions: *Astilbe, ryopteris, Geranium, Filipenula, Ligularia.*

otes: the most important pecies are:

L. nummularia (creeping Jenny), a ground-cover plant for damp soils and riverbanks, growing to only 5–10 cm (2–4 in) and bearing single yellow flowers.

L. punctata grows to 100 cm (40 in) and bears attractive spikes of yellow flowers from June to August. This species is vigorous and spreads extremely fast. The variety *L. punctata* 'Alexander' has foliage spotted with yellowish white.

Blue poppy
Meconopsis species and varieties

❀ 6–9   ⬆ 30–120 (12–48)

Flowers: large, nodding poppy flowers in blue, violet or yellow, soft as silk.

Foliage: light green, elongated ovate, with rough hairs.

Growth habit: rosettes.

Position: soils rich in humus and nutrients, sheltered.

Good companions: *Carex, Hakonechloa macra, Hosta, Kirengeshoma palmata, Matteuccia struthiopteris, Rhododendron.*

Notes: the Himalayan blue poppy (*M. betonicifolia*) grows to 120 cm (48 in), bears cup-shaped, sky-blue flowers, needs plenty of humus and lots of humidity, and makes an excellent companion for rhododendrons. The Welsh poppy (*M. cambrica*) flowers for a very long time (June–September), grows to 30 cm (12 in) and spreads quickly by self-seeding.

Forget-me-not
Myosotis palustris

❀ 5–8   ⬆ 20–30 (8–12)

Flowers: blue forget-me-nots.

51

Foliage: dull green, elongated, with rough hairs.

Growth habit: bushy, puts out runners.

Position: damp garden soils.

Good companions: *Arum, Deschampsia cespitosa, Lysimachia nummularia, Primula*, lady fern.

Blue-eyed Mary
Omphalodes verna

❀ 3–5   ↕ 15–20 (6–8)

Flowers: white or blue, reminiscent of forget-me-nots.

Foliage: fresh green, ovate to heart-shaped, with rough hairs.

Growth habit: spreading ground-cover plant.

Position: humus-rich soils.

Blue-eyed Mary (Omphalodes verna)

Good companions: *Astilbe, Dicentra, Hepatica, Pulmonaria, Waldsteinia*.

Notes: *O. cappadocica* has light-blue flowers from April to May, and spreads only moderately. This species requires open soils. The variety 'Starry Eyes' has blue flowers with white edges.

Phlox divaricata

❀ 4–5   ↕ 20–40 (8–16)

Flowers: lavender-coloured, in umbels, fragrant.

Foliage: matt green, pointed ovate.

Growth habit: clump-forming.

Position: humus-rich garden soils.

Good companions: *Aquilegia, Galium odoratum, Erythronium, Geranium, Trillium*.

Notes: *P. divaricata* 'Dirigo Ice' is a low-growing variety that grows to 30 cm (12 in) and bears blue flowers.

Jacob's ladder
Polemonium caeruleum

❀ 5–6   ↕ 40–80 (16–32)

Flowers: small, lavender-blue bells in loose umbels.

Phlox divaricata

Foliage: fresh green, pinnate, regular arrangement.

Growth habit: dense rosettes

Position: damp soils, includir fairly moist sunny places.

Good companions: *Brunner Campanula, Heuchera*.

Notes: cutting back after flowering promotes growth an leads to a second flowering.

Solomon's seal
Polygonatum × hybridum

❀ 5–6   ↕ 60–90 (24–35)

Flowers: white, tubular, hanging from one side of leaf axils.

Foliage: blue-green, partly shiny, broadly lanceolate.

Growth habit: clump-forming with upright or curved shoots.

Position: open soils rich in humus and nutrients.

Good companions: *Arum*, Japanese anemones, *Hosta*, *Rodgersia*.

Notes: the many-flowered *P. multiflorum* is a native species. It has overhanging stems and white flowers with greenish tips (May–June); height 30–60 cm (12–24 in). See also photo on page 88.

Primrose (Primula vulgaris)

Primula species and varieties

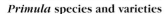

❁ 3–5, 6–8 ⬆ 5–50 (2–20)

Flowers: nearly every colour, trumpet-shaped, single or in umbels or loose racemes.

Foliage: long ovate, in rosettes on the ground.

Growth habit: clump-forming.

Position: soils rich in humus and nutrients.

Good companions: *Asarum*, *Helleborus*, *Hepatica*, *Pulmonaria*, *Myosotis*.

Notes: the most important spring-flowering species are:

• *P. denticulata* (drumstick primula): flowers March–May, height 20–25 cm (8–10 in).

• *P. juliae*: flowers March–April, height 5 cm (2 in), brightly coloured hybrids.

• *P. vulgaris* (primrose): flowers March–April, height 5–10 cm (2–4 in).

• *P. elatior* (oxlip): flowers March– April, height 20 cm (8 in).

The commonest summer-flowering species are:

Drumstick primula (Primula denticulata)

• *P. bulleyana* (candelabra primula): flowers June–August, height 40–50 cm (16–20 in).

• *P. florindae* (giant cowslip): flowers June–July, height 50–60 cm (20–24 in).

Primula × bulleesiana – *a hybrid of* P. beesiana *and* P. bulleyana

Lungwort
Pulmonaria species and varieties

❀ 3–5 ⬆ 20–40 (8–16)

Flowers: red, violet, blue, rarely white, trumpet-shaped, in apical racemes.

Foliage: with rough hairs, often spotted.

Growth habit: clump-forming.

Position: nutrient-rich soils.

Good companions: *Brunnera, Dicentra, Helleborus, Primula, Viola, Waldsteinia.*

Notes: the flowers of *P. angustifolia* (blue cowslip) are carmine-red at first and later azure-blue; the leaves are long

Pulmonaria *'Sissinghurst White'*

and unspotted; 'Alba' has white flowers, while 'Azurea' has gentian-blue flowers.

P. officinalis (lungwort, spotted dog) has pink flowers that turn violet as they begin to wilt.

P. saccharata (Bethlehem sage) has leaves with distinctively large white spots; 'Mrs Moon' has bright-red flowers; those of 'Sissinghurst White' are white.

Rodgersia species and varieties

❀ 6–7 ⬆ 60–120 (24–48)

Flowers: white, reddish, pink or yellowish to greenish-white, in erect or overhanging sprays.

Foliage: dark green, large, rough, palmate or pinnate, with long stems.

Growth habit: bushy, spreads slowly.

Position: soils rich in humus and nutrients.

Good companions: *Aconitum, Actaea, Astilbe, Ligularia,* Japanese anemones, *Rhododendron.*

Notes: some excellent ornamental perennials for shady places:

- *R. aesculifolia* has leaves like those of a horse chestnut, and develops loose, pyramidal sprays of white flowers; height 100 cm (40 in).

Rodgersia

- *R. henrici*: light-blue flowers in 50-cm (20-cm) high sprays
- *R. pinnata:* reddish flowers and shiny dark-green leaves divided into six or nine; height 100 cm (40 in).
- *R. podophylla* grows to 120 cm (48 in) and produces large, overhanging sprays of yellowish-white flowers. *R. podophylla* 'Rotlaub' produces red-brown shoots, while 'Smaragd' is characterised by creamy-white flowers and a broad habit.
- *R. sambucifolia* has pinnate leaves made up of three to five leaflets, and dense sprays of white flowers; height 100 cm (40 in). *R. sambucifolia* 'Rothaut' has dark foliage with red-brown shoots, and grows vigorously.

Saxifrage
Saxifraga species and varieties

🌸 2–10 (mainly 3–6)

🌿 5–60 (2–24)

Flowers: white, less commonly yellow, pink or red, in sprays, racemes or umbels.

Foliage: varies greatly according to species – often moss-like, succulent or in rosettes.

Growth habit: cushion-forming, spreads by runners, sometimes with rosettes, sometimes bushy.

Position: open, humus-rich soils, preferably cool and damp.

London pride

Good companions: *Cyclamen, Festuca, Hyacinthoides, Luzula, Polypodium.*

Notes: saxifrage comes in many different species and varieties, of which the most important include:

- *S. × arendsii*: moss-like cushions; flowers pink, red or white cups with long stems; height 5 cm (2 in).

- *S. fortunei* (syn. *S. cortusifolia* var. *fortunei*): sprays of white flowers in September/October; height 30 cm (12 in); brownish leaves; suitable for sheltered places with humus-rich soil.

- London pride (*S. × urbium*, often sold as *S. umbrosa*): rosettes of dark-green leaves; sprays of fine, pink flowers borne on long stems in May/June; height 20–25 cm (8–10 in).

Comfrey
Symphytum species and varieties

🌸 5–8   🌿 30–60 (12–24)

Flowers: yellow, blue or purple, with rough hairs, tubular, nodding.

Foliage: grey-green, large, ovate, rough hairs.

Comfrey

Growth habit: spreads by means of runners.

Position: humus-rich soils.

Good companions: *Astilbe, Brunnera, Omphalodes verna, Vinca, Waldsteinia.*

Notes: *S. caucasicum* bears azure-blue flowers from June to August.

The creamy-yellow flowers of Turkish comfrey (*S. grandiflorum*) appear as early as May. This species grows vigorously to 25 cm (10 in) and drives out weeds. *S. grandiflorum* 'Goldsmith' has variegated leaves, while 'Hidcote Blue' produces blue flowers that later fade. Both varieties grow to 40 cm (24 in).

Foamflower (Tiarella)

Meadow rue
***Thalictrum* species and varieties**

❀ 5–8 🗡 80–200 (32–80)

Flowers: green, yellow, white or lilac, soft and fragrant with well-developed stamens, in loose or branched sprays.

Foliage: blue-green, pinnate, similar to *Aquilegia*.

Growth habit: upright, clump-forming.

Position: damp to moist, nutrient-rich, preferably acid soils.

Good companions: *Campanula, Carex, Filipendula, Fuchsia, Ligularia*.

Notes: the lilac to purple flowers of *T. aquilegifolium* have such long stamens that they have a feathery appearance;

this native species grows to 120 cm (48 in).

T. flavum has grey-blue tinted foliage and sulphur-yellow flowers, and grows up to 200 cm (80 in) tall.

T. delavayi (syn. *T. dipterocarpum*) has a soft appearance with loose sprays of lilac-tinted flowers; height 120 cm (48 in).

Foamflower
***Tiarella* species**

❀ 4–6 🗡 15–35 (6–14)

Flowers: white, dense but forming loose spikes.

Foliage: lime-green, oval, lobed, reddish autumn colouring.

Growth habit: spreads very gradually, sometimes by means of runners.

Position: humus-rich soils.

Good companions: *Bergenia Carex plantaginea, Dicentra, Pulmonaria, Waldsteinia,* sensitive fern.

Notes: *T. cordifolia* grows to 30 cm (12 in), and produces racemes of white flowers above the foliage in April and May.

The leaves of *T. wherryi* have brown spots near the ground, while their white flowers contain a whiff of pink; this specie grows to 35 cm (14 in) and doesn't produce runners.

***Tradescantia* Andersoniana hybrids**

❀ 5–9 🗡 40–60 (16–24)

Flowers: light blue, violet, rec or white, each with three peta and noticeably yellow stamens in umbels.

Foliage: smooth, grass-like.

Tradescantia

Viola sororia

Growth habit: bushy, clump-forming.

Position: damp, nutrient-rich soils.

Good companions: *Bergenia, Lysimachia, Filipendula, Trollius*.

Globeflower
Trollius europaeus

❀ 5–6 ⬆ 50–70 (20–28)

Flowers: lemon- to marigold-yellow, single, spherical, open cups.

Foliage: fresh green, palmate.

Growth habit: forms dense clumps.

Position: damp, humus- and nutrient-rich soils.

Good companions: *Geranium, Hosta, Omphalodes verna, Pulmonaria, Primula, Thalictrum*.

Periwinkle
Vinca species and varieties

❀ 4–5 ⬆ 10–50 (4–20)

Flowers: violet-blue, purplish-red, lilac or white, star-shaped, single.

Foliage: shiny, broadly lanceolate, evergreen.

Growth habit: broad carpets formed by horizontal shoots.

Position: humus-rich garden soils.

Good companions: *Asarum, Pulmonaria, Helleborus, Actaea, Lamium, Pachysandra*.

Notes: *V. minor* (lesser periwinkle) grows to 15 cm (6 in), with upright flower stems growing clear of foliage. Important varieties include: 'La Grave' syn. 'Bowles Variety' (violet-blue flowers); 'Atropurpurea' syn. 'Rubra' (dark-violet flowers); 'Gertrude Jekyll' (decorative white flowers).

V. major (greater periwinkle) is larger in all respects and grows to 30 cm (12 in) in height. *V. major* 'Variegata' has leaves with white or gold edges.

Lesser periwinkle (Vinca minor)

Violet
Viola species and varieties

❀ 3–8 (*V. odorata* may flower again in September)

⬆ 10–20 (4–8)

Flowers: blue, violet, white, red or yellow, with long spur, standing singly on thin stems.

Foliage: grass-green, broadly heart-shaped.

Growth habit: bushy, spreads by means of runners.

Position: soils rich in humus and nutrients.

Good companions: *Carex, Cyclamen, Galium odoratum, Primula, Pulmonaria*.

Notes: *V. odorata* (sweet violet) has fragrant flowers and develops runners that take root; *V. odorata* 'Queen Charlotte' has dark-violet flowers.

V. sororia (syn. *V. papilonacea*) includes a particularly interesting variety called 'Freckles' that has white flowers speckled with blue.

Waldsteinia

Waldsteinia species

✿ 4–5 🌱 5–25 (2–10)

Flowers: yellow, in dense umbels above foliage.

Foliage: in three to five parts, rough, sometimes hairy, evergreen.

Growth habit: clump-forming or creeping by runners.

Position: garden soils.

Good companions: *Ajuga reptans*, low-growing *Astilbe*, *Hepatica*, *Pulmonaria*, *Viola odorata*.

Notes: *Waldsteinia* is tolerant of root pressure and makes an ideal ground-cover plant, absorbing fallen leaves and repelling weeds. *W. geoides* has lovely autumn colouring, but forms clumps without runners and establishes itself more slowly than *W. ternata* with its creeping runners.

Grasses for shady places

Grasses, with their many interesting characteristics, have earned a special place in shady gardens. Their long leaf blades are particularly effective, adding to the interplay of different patterns.

Grasses can also enrich the garden design by making it less formal and more varied. The patterns on their leaves, combined with their very modest flowers, stand in bold contrast to the much larger flowers borne by most perennials and bulb plants.

Carex morrowii *'Variegata' looks particularly effective in the autumn.*

Sedge
Carex species and varieties

✿ 5–8 🌱 10–70 (4–28)

Flowers: light-yellow, green or red-brown, loosely hanging upright to brush-like ears 15–100 cm (6–40 in) long.

Leaves: stiff, shiny, fresh to dark green, often with marking in other colours, evergreen.

Growth habit: loose or dense clumps.

Position: humus-rich, loamy to damp soils.

Good companions: *Epimedium*, *Galanthus*, *Pulmonaria*, *Rhododendron*, *Tiarella*.

Notes: mace sedge (*C. grayi*) has interesting ears that are

Descahmpsia cespitosa *(tufted hair grass)*

reminiscent of stars; growth height 30–60 cm (12–24 in); flowers July–August.

C. morrowii 'Variegata', with its yellow-edged evergreen leaves, is ideal for planting under trees; height 40 cm (16 in); flowers June–July.

C. oshimensis 'Evergold' (syn. *C. morrowii* 'Evergold') has leaves with gold or white stripes; it is evergreen; growth height 20–30 cm (8–12 in); flowers May.

Pendulous sedge (*C. pendula*) grows to 100 cm (40 in) and produces long, overhanging ears in June.

C. plantaginea is noted for its broad, light-green evergreen leaves; growth height 20–30 cm (8–12 in); flowers April/May.

Tufted hair grass
Deschampsia cespitosa

❀ 6–8 ⬆ 30–60 (12–24)

Flowers: veil-like, yellowish-brown sprays growing to 70–100 cm (28–40 in).

Leaves: flat, overhanging, fresh green; golden-yellow autumn colouring.

Growth habit: dense clumps.

Position: damp, nutrient-rich soils.

Good companions: *Aquilegia, Astilbe, Campanula, Hosta*.

Notes: *D. cespitosa* 'Tauträger' has soft sprays of flowers that emerge late in the summer.

Festuca gautieri
(syn. *F. scoparia*)

❀ 6–7 ⬆ 10–15 (4–6)

Flowers: thin, yellowish-green sprays, 15–25 cm (6–10 in) tall.

Leaves: juicy, green, fine stems, evergreen.

Growth habit: thick cushions.

Position: poor, open soils.

Good companions: *Chionodoxa, Crocus tommasinianus, Heuchera, Scilla*.

Notes: *F. gautieri* 'Pic Carlit' is very pretty and compact, and suitable for pots.

Hakonechloa macra

❀ 7–10 ⬆ 30–40 (12–16)

Flowers: greenish ears, elegant-looking, 30–40 cm (12–16 in) tall.

Leaves: dark green, lanceolate, overhanging.

Growth habit: clump-forming, with runners.

Position: humus-rich soils; in a pot, tolerates short periods of dryness.

Good companions: *Dryopteris erythrosora*, low-growing *Hosta, Primula*.

Notes: *H. macra* 'Aureola' (see photo below) is well known for

Hakonechloa macra *'Aureola'*

its green-and-yellow-striped leaves and grows up to 60 cm (24 in) in height. Both the species and the variety look particularly good when planted among smaller specimens, and are also very suitable for growing in pots.

Woodrush
Luzula species

❀ 4–7   🌡 10–30 (4–12)

Flowers: white, borne on umbel-like sprays 20–40 cm (8–16 in) tall.

Leaves: dark green, shiny, broadly lineal, evergreen, appearing early.

Growth habit: clump-forming, wide-spreading.

Position: open, damp, lime-free, humus-rich soils.

Snowy woodrush (Luzula nivea)

Northern maidenhair fern (Adiantum pedatum)

Good companions: *Epimedium, Heuchera, Hosta, Tiarella, Vinca, Waldsteinia*.

Notes: *L. nivea* (snowy woodrush) produces lots of white flowers on umbel-like sprays.

L. pilosa has brown, umbel-like flowers.

The *L. sylvatica* (greater woodrush) is evergreen and produces thick sprays of brown flowers from April to June.

All species make reliable, easy-care ground-cover plants.

Ferns for shady places

Ferns make wonderfully decorative foliage plants for shady places. These unusual, rather primaeval-looking plants are fond of light shade, and don't like extreme conditions. They don't have any beautiful flowers, but their elegant fronds come in many interesting and varied forms, making them ideal candidates for planting under solitary trees or along hedgerows.

orthern maidenhair fern
diantum pedatum

40–60 (16–24)

eaves: finely divided, light-
reen fronds on wiry black
ems.

rowth habit: broad, slowly
oreading clumps.

osition: acid, humus-rich
oils, humid air and protection
rom late frosts.

ood companions: *Cyclamen,*
eucojum, Luzula sylvatica,
rimula, Tiarella, Trillium,
ow-growing *Rhododendron.*

ady fern (Athyrium filix-femina)

Lady fern
Athyrium filix-femina

↑ 40–100 (16–40)

Leaves: large, finely divided,
light-green fronds.

Growth habit: densely bushy,
short rhizomes.

Position: damp or dampish,
lime-free soils.

Good companions: *Brunnera*
macrophylla, Carex morrowii,
Primula.

Notes: *A. nipponicum* (painted
fern) has fronds with a metallic
shimmer (height 30–40 cm/
12–16 in). *A. nipponicum* var.
pictum also has silvery-grey
markings on its leaves.

Hard fern
Blechnum spicant

↑ 20–50 (8–20)

Leaves: simple fronds, leathery,
evergreen.

Growth habit: rhizomes with
runners.

Position: damp, acid, humus-
rich soils, humid air.

Good companions: *Asarum,*
Epimedium, Polygonatum,
Primula, azalea.

Notes: native species, ideal for
natural-looking designs.

Chinese holly fern (Cyrtomium fortunei)

Chinese holly fern
Cyrtomium fortunei (syn.
Polystichum falcatum var.
fortunei)

↑ 40–70 (16–28)

Leaves: dark-green fronds,
simple, firm, leathery and
pointed.

Growth habit: upright in
layers, clump-forming.

Position: lime-free soils; needs
to be protected from wind and
winter sun; tolerates dryness.

Good companions: *Carex*
morrowii, Deschampsia cespi-
tosa, Rhododendron, box.

Dryopteris *(buckler fern)*

Buckler fern
Dryopteris species

⬆ 40–140 (16–56)

Leaves: shiny green, triangular, simple to doubly-compound fronds, very decorative growth.

Growth habit: upright or trumpet-shaped, sometimes gently overhanging or spreading.

Position: humus-rich soils.

Good companions: *Anemone nemorosa, Deschampsia cespitosa, Galanthus, Vinca, Pulmonaria.*

Notes: *D. affinis* has golden-brown scales on its stems and on newly sprouting fronds.

The Japanese shield fern (*D. erythrosora*) has red-brown stems that look like newly sprouting fronds.

The male fern (*D. filix-mas*) is one of the largest of our native ferns, growing up to 140 cm (56 in) in height.

Oak fern
Gymnocarpium dryopteris

⬆ 10–30 (4–12)

Leaves: soft, light-green fronds, forming symmetrical triangles.

Growth habit: carpet-forming, spreading by means of runners.

Position: humus-rich soils.

Good companions: *Aquilegia, Cyclamen coum, Luzula.*

Notes: good ground-cover plant.

Matteuccia struthiopteris *is known as the ostrich fern or shuttlecock fern.*

Ostrich fern, shuttlecock fern
Matteuccia struthiopteris

⬆ 80–120 (32–48)

Leaves: fresh-green compound fronds, sprouting early; fertile spore fronds, coloured olive-green to dark brown, sprouting from inside the trumpet.

Growth habit: shuttlecock-shaped, opening out into a vase-like shape as the season progresses; rootstock spreads by means of runners.

Position: soils rich in humus and nutrients.

Good companions: *Brunnera, Hosta, Rodgersia, Waldsteinia.*

Sensitive fern
Onoclea sensibilis

⬆ 40–50 (16–20)

Leaves: simple fresh-green fronds that sprout pale red; erect; light-brown spore fronds in the centre.

Growth habit: vigorous creeping rhizome.

Position: damp, humus-rich soils.

Good companions: *Carex grayi, Hosta, Lysimachia nummularia, Primula.*

Notes: ideal for planting on shaded riverbanks.

Royal fern
Osmunda regalis

⬆ 60–140 (24–56)

Leaves: light-green compound fronds, bright-yellow autumn colouring.

Growth habit: clump-forming, trumpet-shaped.

Position: damp, nutritious, lime-free soils, humid air and mild winters.

Good companions: *Arum, Aruncus, Carex pendula, Hosta, Rodgersia.*

Notes: the fronds of *O. regalis* 'purpurascens' sprout purple

Royal fern (Osmunda regalis)

and turn purple again in the autumn; height 60–140 cm (24–56 in).

Hart's-tongue fern
Asplenium scolopendrium
syn. *Phyllitis scolopendrium*

⬆ 20–40 (8–16)

Leaves: simple tongue-shaped fronds, shiny dark green with black midrib, evergreen.

Growth habit: broad, clump-forming.

Position: damp soils rich in nutrients and humus.

Good companions: *Adiantum pedatum, Galium odoratum, Polygonatum.*

Notes: plant needs protection from winter sun.

Common polypody
Polypodium vulgare

⬆ 20–30 (8–12)

Leaves: simple fronds, gently overhanging, evergreen.

Growth habit: carpet-forming.

Position: lime-free, sandy or gritty soils with thin humus layer.

Good companions: *Festuca gautieri, Saxifraga, Vinca.*

Notes: suitable for alpine gardens or the tops of walls.

Hart's-tongue fern

Shield fern
Polystichum species and varieties

⬆ 40–100 (16–40)

Leaves: dull-green fronds in graceful curves, usually evergreen, very decorative.

Growth habit: forms an upright clump.

Position: cool, damp, nutrient-rich soils with good drainage, humid air.

Good companions: *Actaea, Anemone, Euphorbia amygdaloides* var. *robbiae, Helleborus.*

Notes: shield ferns add extra colour to the winter scene. They also help to protect many

Soft shield fern (Polystichum setiferum)

Glory-of-the-snow gone wild

spring-flowering plants, for which they also provide an excellent backdrop.

P. aculeatum (hard shield fern) produces elegantly curved fronds that remain green right through into the spring; height 40–70 cm (16–28 in).

P. setiferum (soft shield fern) grows to 1 m (40 in) and forms graceful, gently spreading fronds with a diameter of 1.2 m (4 ft). It comes in several different forms, such as Divisilobum, also known as 'Proliferum' (finely divided dark-green fronds, evergreen, height 70 cm/28 in), and Divisilobum 'Dahlem', also known as 'Proliferum Dahlem' (young fronds bright green; height 40 cm/16 in).

Bulb plants for shady places

Bulb plants are particularly important in the garden during the first half of the year. Tiny plants such as squill (*Scilla*) and snowdrop (*Galanthus*) come into their own in the early spring before the leaves appear on the trees, and die back into the soil before summer has even begun.

The bulb usually consists of a swollen underground bud. It serves chiefly as a storage organ for nutrients, enabling growth to begin during the winter, and providing extra reserves for both flowers and leaves to grow.

Glory-of-the-snow
Chionodoxa luciliae

 3–4   ⬆ 10–20 (4–8)

Flowers: blue, star-shaped, usually white in the centre, in loose racemes.

Foliage: grass-green, lineal.

Growth habit: spreading.

Position: nutrient-rich soils under open shrubs, dry in summer.

Good companions: *Cyclamen, Eranthis hyemalis, Polypodium*.

Notes: spreads by self-seeding; each raceme holds up to 12 nodding flowers, which are blue with a white background; height up to 15 cm (6 in).

C. luciliae 'Gigantea' has larger leaves and flowers than the species.

Cyclamen coum

C. luciliae 'Alba' has pure-white upright flowers; height 10 cm (4 in).

Crocus tommasinianus

 2–3   ⬆ 8–12 (3–5)

Flowers: trumpet-shaped, pale violet.

Foliage: fine, grass-like.

Growth habit: self-seeds gradually to form ever-larger colonies.

Position: damp to moderately dry soils.

Good companions: *Cyclamen, Eranthis hyemalis, Galanthus*.

Notes: ideal for colonising the space under solitary shrubs such as magnolia or Japanese maple.

Cyclamen species

 2–4/7–11   ⬆ 8–12 (3–5)

Flowers: pink, white or carmine-red; distinctive *Cyclamen* flowers.

Foliage: heart-shaped, round or kidney-shaped, often with whitish-grey markings.

Growth habit: grows from a flat tuber that becomes continually larger with age; self-seeds to form colonies.

Erythronium

Position: open, lime-rich soils, dry in summer.

Good companions: *Crocus, Galanthus*.

Notes: *C. coum* flowers from February to April.

C. purpurascens flowers from July to August.

C. hederifolium flowers from August to November and has evergreen leaves similar to those of ivy.

Erythronium species and varieties

 3–5   ⬆ 15–40 (6–16)

Flowers: white, yellow or pink to dark pink; hanging gracefully; a certain resemblance to the margaton lily.

Foliage: green, lanceolate, sometimes variegated.

Growth habit: clump-forming.

Position: open, humus-rich soils.

Good companions: *Aquilegia, Galanthus, Primula.*

Notes: *E. dens-canis* (dog's-tooth violet) has blue-green leaves with dark spots and readily naturalises; height 15–20 cm (6–8 in).

E. 'Pagoda', the most popular variety, has bronze markings on its leaves and produces sulphur-yellow flowers in April and May; height 30–40 cm (12–16 in).

Snake's-head fritillary
Fritillaria meleagris

❀ 3–6 🗍 20–30 (8–12)

Flowers: bell-shaped, with checkerboard pattern of pink to purple with white.

Foliage: grass-green, grass-like.

Snake's-head fritillary (Fritillaria meleagris)

Growth habit: single shoot, spreads by means of offsets.

Position: soils rich in humus and nutrients.

Good companions: *Carex pendula, Dryopteris, Leucojum vernum.*

Notes: several related species also do well in light shade:

- *F. camschatcensis* (black sarana) develops a single erect shoot and bears dark-violet flowers from May to June; height 15–35 cm (6–14 in).

- The bell-shaped flowers of *F. michailovskyi* are purplish-brown outside and yellow inside, and appear in April; height 15 cm (6 in).

- *F. pallidiflora* produces long, pale-yellow bells in April; height 30–40 cm (6–8 in).

Common snowdrop
Galanthus nivalis

❀ 2–4 🗍 10–15 (4–6)

Flowers: white with green markings, bell-shaped, fragrant.

Foliage: dark-green, narrowly lineal.

Growth habit: forms loose clumps, spreading.

Position: damp, humus-rich soils.

English bluebell (Hyacinthoides non-scripta)

Good companions: *Crocus tommasinianus, Cyclamen coum, Eranthis hyemalis, Hepa[...] ica, Rhododendron praecox.*

Notes: the seeds are spread by ants. *G. elwesii* has larger leave[s] and flowers, which appear as early as January; height 15–20 cm (6–8 in). The double flowe[rs] of *G. nivalis* 'Flore Pleno' are particularly attractive; height 10–15 cm (4–6 in).

Spanish bluebell
Hyacinthoides hispanica

❀ 5–6 🗍 20–40 (8–16)

Flowers: mid-blue to violet-blue, bell-shaped, in spherical sprays.

Foliage: grass-green, broadly lineal.

Growth habit: rosette-shaped clumps, forms loose colonies.

Position: humus-rich soils.

Good companions: *Galium odoratum, Pulmonaria, Waldsteinia, Rhododendron.*

Notes: the Spanish bluebell comes in a large number of varieties, most of which are distinguished by their flower colour (including pink and white).

The English bluebell (*H. non-cripta*) is very popular in woodland gardens. It flowers in May and spreads to form broad carpets.

Spring snowflake
Leucojum vernum

✿ 2–4   🔸 15–20 (6–8)

Flowers: white bells with yellowish-green spots at the tip,

Spring snowflake (Leucojum vernum)

fragrant, only one flower on each stem.

Foliage: fresh green, strap-shaped.

Growth habit: forms loose colonies.

Position: humus-rich soils.

Good companions: *Carex pendula, Helleborus, Hosta,* lady fern.

Notes: the closely related summer snowflake (*L. aesti-vum*) produces flowers from May to June, with several flowers on each shoot, which can grow up to 60 cm (24 in) high.

Siberian squill
Scilla siberica

✿ 3–4   🔸 10–15 (4–6)

Flowers: azure-blue, star-shaped, in racemes.

Foliage: grass-green, broadly lineal.

Growth habit: carpet-forming.

Position: humus-rich soils.

Good companions: *Carex umbrosa, Dryopteris, Epimedi-um, Tiarella, Leucojum vernum.*

Notes: self-seeds; the lesser-known *S. bifolia* is smaller in all respects but flowers earlier.

Birthroot (Trillium erectum)

Woodlily
Trillium species

✿ 4–5   🔸 20–40 (8–16)

Flowers: pink, white or wine-red, in whorls of three, upright to nodding.

Foliage: in whorls of three, with bracts immediately below flowers, sometimes spotted.

Growth habit: loose clumps.

Position: humus-rich soils.

Good companions: *Anemone nemorosa, Carex umbrosa, Dryopteris, Helleborus, Hosta.*

Notes: *T. erectum* (birthroot): green-and-red flowers; height 30–40 cm (12–16 in). *T. grandi-florum* (wake robin): striking pure-white flowers; height 20–40 cm (8–16 in). *T. sessile* is noted for its variegated foliage and burgundy-red flowers.

As a ground-cover plant, creeping dogwood is good for underplanting.

Shrubs for shady places

Bushes give structure to plantings in the shade. If the shade is not caused by buildings or trees, then shrubs make essential companions for herbaceous plants.

Evergreen foliage plants provide an excellent backdrop for lighter-coloured flowers, while flowering shrubs blend harmoniously with the other plants.

Some shrubs even make robust ground-cover plants that are easy to maintain.

Creeping dogwood
Cornus canadensis

❀ 5–6 ⬆ 10–20 (4–8)

Flowers: tiny, greenish-red, each surrounded by four white bracts up to 3 cm (1 in) across.

Foliage: pointed ovate, deeply lined.

Growth habit: shallow, spreading ground-cover plant.

Position: open, damp, slightly acid soils.

Good companions: *Festuca*, *Heuchera*, dwarf azalea, hart's-tongue fern.

Notes: ideal for underplanting.

Common ivy
Hedera helix

❀ 9–10 ⬆ climbing to 800 (320), creeping 10–20 (4–8)

Flowers: compact umbels of round, greenish-yellow flower only appearing on older plant (i.e. after about ten years).

Fruits: shiny black berries.

Foliage: triangular, lobed, leathery, evergreen, becoming roundish or rhomboid with ag

Growth habit: creeping or climbing by means of aerial roots, needing a rough surface in order to cling.

Position: undemanding but prefers humus-rich soils.

Good companions: *Geraniu Hydrangea*, *Luzula sylvatica*, *Vinca*, box, yew.

Notes: variegated leaves requi more light than green. The leaves of *H. helix* 'Goldheart' are pale yellow in the centre. 'Woerner' grows vigorously by up to 150 cm (60 in) a year.

Hydrangea species and varieties

❀ 6–10 ⬆ 100–300 (40–12

Flowers: white, red and blue, flat to spherical sprays with lo of individual flowers.

oliage: large, ovate, evergreen.

Growth habit: broadly bushy.

Position: damp, humus-rich oils.

Good companions: *Astilbe*, *Hosta*, ferns, grasses.

Notes: *H. arborescens* has balls of white flowers measuring 6–9 cm (2.5–3.5 in) across; height 100–200 cm (40–80 in).

H. aspera sargentiana has hairy leaves and large sprays measuring 7–9 cm (3–3.5 in) across; height 300 cm (120 in).

H. macrophylla comes in many varieties, with blue, pink and white flowers in balls or flat sprays (6–10 cm/2.5–4 in); height 100–150 cm (40–60 in).

Hydrangea aspera sargentiana

Rose of Sharon (Hypericum calycinium)

Acid soils and aluminium sulphate, often called a hydrangea colorant, should enhance the colour of blue flowers.

Rose of Sharon
Hypericum calycinum

✿ 7–9   ⬆ 20–30 (8–12)

Flowers: golden-yellow cups with long stamens.

Foliage: dark green, elongated ovate, evergreen.

Growth habit: carpet-forming sub-shrub (basal stems woody).

Position: moderately dry to damp soils.

Good companions: *Berberis*, *Geranium*, *Spiraea*, yew.

Notes: the following are also suited to sunless or shady positions: *H.* 'Hidcote' (flowers July to October; height 80–150 cm/ 32–60 in) and *H. androsaemum* (June to August; 100 cm/40 in).

Honeysuckle
Lonicera species and varieties

✿ 5–7   ⬆ 80–300 (32–120)

Flowers: white, yellow, red or pink, usually tubular, arranged in pairs or whorls.

Fruits: blue, black or red berries, usually round to flat.

Foliage: broadly ovate, dull green, early-sprouting; topmost leaf pairs fused at base.

Growth habit: broadly upright to spreading or climbing.

Position: garden soils.

Good companions: *Dicentra*, *Lamium*, *Tradescantia*.

Lonicera × heckrottii

Pachysandra terminalis

Notes: among the species suited to shade are *L. pericly-menum* (common honeysuckle, woodbine) and the evergreen *L. henryi*. If supported, both species will grow to 200–300 cm (80–120 in). *L. henryi* bears small yellowish-red flowers in June and July, followed later by black berries. *L. periclymenum* produces fragrant yellowish-red flowers from June to September, and its fruits are red.

Half-shade is suitable for *L. × brownii* (scarlet trumpet honey-suckle), which bears orange-red flowers from June to September (height 200–300 cm/80–120 in), and *L. × heckrottii* (purple and yellowish-white flowers from June to October; height 200–500 cm/80–200 in).

Pachysandra terminalis

❀ 4–5　❦ 20–30 (8–12)

Flowers: white, in erect spikes.

Foliage: toothed, rhomboid, leathery, evergreen.

Growth habit: mat-forming sub-shrub, slow-growing, develops runners.

Position: humus-rich, slightly acid soils.

Good companions: *Campanula*, *Dryopteris*, *Hydrangea*, *Lamium*, *Rhododendron*, box.

Notes: mats can be rejuvenated by cutting back radically using a lawnmower with the blades set high.

Rhododendron, azalea
Rhododendron species and varieties

❀ 5–6, depending on variety

❦ depends on variety; 120–35 (45–140) large-flowered hybri

Flowers: tight clusters in man different colours, up to 20 cm (8 in) across.

Growth habit: bushy to broa ly spherical, usually compact.

Position: open, lime-free, humus-rich soils with plenty o moisture but well-drained.

Good companions: *Hosta*, *Pachysandra*, *Primula bulley ana*, lady fern, yew.

Notes: see table opposite.

Various rhododendrons in bloom

Rhododendrons and azaleas

Species or variety	Height (cm/in)	Flowering season / description of flowers	Growth habit	Notes
Large-flowered rhododendrons	150–200 (60–80)	May to June / large flowers, white, pink, lilac, yellow or red according to variety, some with a spot in the flower	broadly bushy, loose	recommended varieties: 'Blattgold' (spotted foliage), 'Furnivall's Daughter' (pink flowers with dark spot), 'Nova Zembla' (ruby-red)
R. williamsianum	100–150 (40–60)	May / pink or red, bell-shaped	broadly upright, dense foliage	needs sheltered position
R. forrestii repens	40–60 (16–24)	May / scarlet	bushy, dwarf species	sheltered position, ideal for riverbanks
R. yakushimanum **hybrids**	100–150 (40–60)	May–June / dense balls of pink, red, yellow or white flowers	compact, semi-spherical, dense foliage	hairy leaves, tolerant of sunshine, flowers very readily
R. impeditum	20–40 (8–16)	April–May / soft, violet-blue flowers	bushy, flat	ideal for small gardens
R. **'Praecox'**	100–150 (40–60)	February–April / lilac-pink	loosely upright	harbinger of spring, looks good with winter heather and snowdrops
Large-flowered azaleas	100–150 (40–60)	May–June / pink, red, orange, yellow, sometimes fragrant	loosely upright	deciduous, intense colours, flowers look good from a distance
Japanese azaleas	100–150 (40–60)	May–June / pink, red, white, orange-red	compact evergreen	azaleas (dwarf varieties) max. 100 cm (40 in)

Rhododendron 'Mrs Furnivall'

Common yew
Taxus baccata

 3–4 🌡 500–700 (200–280)

Flowers: small; yellow male flowers, insignificant female flowers.

Fruit: berry-like, with red, fleshy mantle enclosing grey kernel (highly poisonous).

Foliage: the shiny, dark-green needles are evergreen and also poisonous.

Growth habit: bushy, loosely branching.

Position: nutrient-rich soils, adaptable.

Good companions: *Actaea, Carex morrowii, Digitalis,* Japanese anemones, *Lonicera.*

Notes: slow-growing, tolerant of pruning.

Planting and maintenance

areful planning and thorough preparation of the soil should
garantee success at planting in the shade. You will soon be
ble to create a harmonious balance between the different
ants, and after that a few simple but regular tasks are all that
required to keep the beds in order.

The area beneath this pine tree has been colonised by Cyclamen hederifolium, *with flower colours that vary between light and dark pink.*

nce you have made a list of
eas and suggestions, the first
ing to consider is the local
tuation, as this has to be
ited to the requirements of
e plants if you are going to
cceed.

The two main factors to con-
der are the light conditions
nd the state of the soil.

he local situation

efore getting out paper and
en, or going out with your
heelbarrow and spade, the
rst thing you must do is to
ssess the local conditions. The
vo main tasks involved here
re an exact assessment of the
inds of shade to be found in
our garden and a thorough
xamination of the soil
onditions.

*Regular thinning of trees and shrubs
mproves the light conditions.
erbaceous perennials should be
runed in the autumn.*

The light conditions

We have already looked at the
different types of shade (see
page 8 ff.). Now is the time to
apply this knowledge to your
own garden, taking account of
both the daily and the seasonal
changes. The following factors
need to be taken into account:

- Is the area shaded by trees or
  shrubs, or by buildings?

- Are any trees or shrubs on
  your land or on that of your
  neighbour?

- Do you know what species
  they are? If they are evergreen, for example, they will
  give shade in the winter as
  well as the summer.

- If they are deciduous, when
  do they start to produce
  leaves?

- How much do they grow in a
  year?

- How does the light change
  during the course of the day
  and/or during the course of
  the year?

Improving the light conditions

If the area is shaded by trees or
shrubs, then you should consider pruning them before you
start planting – for two reasons:
first, it will be easier to do this
without damaging the beds
below, and secondly, the extra
light provided will give the
young plants a better start.

But you will also need to take
the shrubs themselves into
account. While most bushy
shrubs are tolerant of pruning,
there are some trees and shrubs
that will lose their distinctive
form, especially those that are
slow-growing or have been

73

It can be very helpful to get an exact idea of how much shade is being cast by trees and shrubs, and to keep tabs on them especially during the flowering and fruiting seasons. If these plants drop flower petals in the early summer, or fruits in the high summer, then you should never plant large-leaved perennials close by, because if the falling petals or fruits are wet, they will stick to the foliage of plants such as *Hosta*. On the other hand, they will pass easily between finely divided leaves such as those possessed by *Astilbe* or grasses.

grafted. Moreover, not all trees will grow back again after pruning. Conifers in particular can be problematic.

Only a few shrubs will survive radical pruning without sustaining at least some damage. The remaining rootstock will quickly put out side-shoots, but these in turn will need to be trained. For example, a hazelnut bush that originally had two or three decent-sized stems will now put out ten times as many shoots. Even the thinnest of branches will grow strongly, and the end result of all this will be a dense thicket.

Thinning is therefore much more sensible than radical pruning. Bushy shrubs can be thinned from the bottom upwards, starting with old branches that can be cut off at their point of origin. From this point of view, thinning is also a rejuvenating process.

With a full-size tree, the crown can be similarly thinned. If major branches are each cut back to the branching point, the side branches will take over their role and grow more vigorously. The plant will look rather bare at first, but it will soon regain its shape as new shoots appear with the first leaves.

Legal requirements for pruning trees and shrubs

Before you start cutting and sawing, you will need to check the legality of what you intend to do.

With trees and shrubs along the boundary of your land, you don't need your neighbour's permission to remove anything that is growing over their land, but it's best to enlist their co-operation for the sake of good neighbourliness. If you want to cut back a neighbour's tree that is overhanging your land, you may do so provided you offer

them the prunings, including any fruit.

Before going ahead, though you should contact your local planning authority to see if there is a preservation order your trees (in which case thei permission is required) or if you live in a Conservation Are (in which case you will need give them notice).

Pruning may involve other conservation issues such as th possible effect on nesting son birds or bats (which are legall protected). If you cut a hedge back too early in the year, you run the risk of killing the your

Rhododendrons thrive in the shade o tall trees. If you remove single branch es, more light will penetrate to the lower layers.

Improving the light in the shade of buildings

There is no way of reducing the shade of buildings, but there are ways of improving the light indirectly.

The reflected light from a wall makes a great difference, so you can paint it in a light colour that matches both the rest of the building and the colours of the plants you intend to have. A 50-cm (20-in) band of a darker colour along the bottom of a wall will prevent any muddy splashes from showing – or alternatively you could run a 30-cm (12-in) wide gravel path along between the wall and the flower beds.

The state of the soil

There are various ways of examining the soil. At one extreme you could have a soil sample tested professionally at a laboratory, which would provide such information as the balance of nutrients and the pH value.

A cheaper alternative, however, might be to test the soil yourself using one of the kits available from specialist outlets or garden centres. If you do this, it's important to follow the accompanying instructions exactly.

Simple but helpful – the finger test

There are two classic tests that gardeners use to check the soil: the finger test, and observation of wild vegetation.

To do a finger test, first put your spade into the ground and remove a little of the soil. You can already tell a lot from just looking at the soil. If it's dark, this suggests a high level of humus, while light-coloured soil is likely to contain large amounts of sand or loam. If there are a lot of stones, these will naturally make a noise against the spade.

The finger test is extremely simple, although it needs to be done carefully. You just take a little soil in your hand, and try to roll it into little balls:

- If the soil rolls easily into firm balls, this suggests a high proportion of **clay**, which means that it will compact very readily and won't drain very well.

- If any balls that are formed quickly break up and leave a floury deposit between your fingers, then you are dealing with **silty soil**.

- If the soil refuses to roll into balls, then it contains a lot of **sand**.

Adding well-rotted garden compost not only improves the nutrient levels in the soil but also enriches it with valuable humus. It thus improves both drainage and the aeration, and also activates the soil fauna.

Improving the soil

How to improve the soil will depend on what it is like in the first place. The basic aim is to improve aeration and drainage in relation to water retention, and thus to avoid extremes.

A **dense, clay soil** is made up of a large number of very fine particles, and can be improved by adding something with much coarser particles. Sand is what is usually added in practice.

75

Sandy soils are lacking in fine particles, which means that they cannot retain much water. Adding loam to the sand is not a practical solution. The usual method is to resort to that all-round soil improver known as **humus**. This contains lots of plant fibres that store water, while at the same time activating the tiny creatures that live in the soil.

Humus is also recommended for **loamy** or **silty soils**, especially in the shade. Most shade plants come from deciduous woodlands, where they thrive on humus-rich soils.

The pH level

The pH level is an important factor for shade plants. Rhodo-dendrons and moorland or bogland plants prefer an acid soil (i.e. with a pH value of under 7). The best way to achieve this is to add plenty of humus and avoid lime or chalk.

Typical woodland plants such as *Corydalis* or *Hepatica* prefer an alkaline soil (i.e. with a pH value of more than 7). These plants need humus that has been mixed with lime.

Preparing the soil

Before you start planting, you need to dig the soil over to open it up. Ideally it should be dug over to about a spade's depth, taking care not to damage any tree roots. This is also the best time for adding any further ingredients such as sand and grit, or humus. It's best to leave the soil to rest afterwards so that it can settle and regain its structure.

If you're planting in the early spring, you can also combine soil preparation with fertilising so as to give the plants a good start. Plenty of light and nutrients are needed for early growth.

Ground elder and other weeds

Weeds are among the least-popular garden plants, whether in the shade or in the sun. While preparing the soil you should also get rid of all weed roots. This is admittedly a very exhausting task, but it will be very much worth the effort in the long run, provided you carry it out consistently.

Ground elder (*Aegopodium podagraria*) is a vigorous weed that is especially fond of the shade – no corner is too dark for it. You should take great care to remove every trace of this plant, whether root, rhizome or stolon. If an area is particularly badly affected, it's worth leaving it after a first digging-over so that any parts you have missed can sprout

Before planting Christmas roses (Helleborus niger), *you will need to add lime to the soil. However, Lenten roses* (H. orientalis) *and other hellebores will thrive in neutral or even slightly acid soils.*

Ground elder has to be completely eradicated with the help of a fork, because even the smallest piece of a root will sprout again.

gain – then you can remove them completely before you start planting.

Humus – essential for shade plants

Humus consists predominantly of dead organic material, mainly from plants but also from animal remains. It is being continually broken down in the soil by micro-organisms, and this is what produces the characteristics that are so important for growth: an open structure, a high soil temperature and a plentiful but well-balanced supply of nutrients.

Humus plays an important role in gardening because it is so fertile. Shade without humus is difficult to imagine, because the soil under trees becomes covered with leaves or needles, creating a permanent layer of humus for the plants that grow under the trees.

The simplest way of improving humus levels is to allow the autumn leaves to remain on the flower beds. Possible additives include well-rotted garden compost, bark compost or other plant remains such as coir (coconut fibre).

The breakdown of nutrients is assisted by lime and nitrogen, so lime- or nitrogen-rich fertilisers are also recommended (the soil nutrients must first be broken down so that the plants can absorb them).

Soil with roots in

The soil under trees with horizontal roots such as pines (*Pinus*) or birches (*Betula*), or under old, established trees, is full of roots that can make it difficult for herbaceous plants to get a proper foothold. This soil receives only a small amount of rainwater, and the delicate young plants with their tiny roots can often be starved

of essential water and nutrients by the much stronger tree roots.

The best way to solve this problem is by adding an extra 15–20-cm (6–8-in) layer of fresh garden soil underneath the tree. Then the perennials and ground-cover plants soon develop firm roots in the fresh, open soil.

Dealing with compacted soil

Any kind of soil is liable to become compacted, especially during the preparation phase, simply because you are stepping on it. As soil in the shade tends to hold a lot of water, any compaction is likely to cause further problems later on.

One way to remove the last traces of ground elder (*Aegopodium podagraria*) from a bed with nothing else is to cover the whole area with a sheet of black plastic mulch. Any remaining roots will sprout, but the plants will soon die from lack of light. You will, however, need to be very patient, as it takes about four weeks for this obstinate plant to finish sprouting.

The best way to avoid soil
compaction is to introduce
paving slabs or stepping stones.
Wooden discs are often used in
woodland gardens, but they
soon become slippery in wet
weather. You can, however,
cover them with wire netting to
stop you slipping. Stepping
stones, on the other hand, will
quickly become surrounded by
the leaves of perennials, and
will soon blend in harmoniously with the plants.

*Stepping stones are a good way of
improving access to large flower beds,
and help prevent you from compacting
the soil underfoot.*

*This natural-looking planting brings variety into the garden. Remember that wide
planting distances give your plants plenty of room to develop, and any gaps will
soon be filled.*

Buying plants

When buying plants, always
make sure that you're buying
healthy, good-quality specimens. You can be certain of this
if they have strong shoots and a
well-established root ball. A
good plant should also have
buds during the flowering
season. If there are buds outside the plant's normal flowering season and the plant gives a
rather miserable impression,
then leave well alone. This is a
sign of 'emergency flowering'
and will further weaken the

plant. The pot should also be
labelled to indicate what the
plant is, unless of course there
is a label stuck in the soil.

Planting density

When planting out, you need
make sure the plants are the
right distance apart. The fresh
planted bed will look rather
bare at first, but the plants will
soon spread to occupy the
space as the growth season ge
underway. If you plant them
too close together, they will
soon be crowding each other

Planting densities for the most important shade plants

Planting density	Plant name (including botanical name)	Planting density	Plant name (including botanical name)
1–3 plants per m² (sq yd)	*Actaea cordifolia* (syn. *Cimicifuga racemosa* var. *cordifolia*)	9–12 plants per m² (sq yd)	Northern maidenhair fern (*Adiantum pedatum*)
	Actaea dahurica (syn. *Cimicifuga dahurica*)		Hart's-tongue fern (*Asplenium scolopendrium* syn. *Phyllitis scolopendrium*)
	Actaea racemosa (syn. *Cimicifuga racemosa*)		*Astilbe chinensis* var. *pumila*
	Goatsbeard (*Aruncus dioicus*)		*Astilbe japonica*
	Lady fern, painted fern (*Athyrium* species)		*Astilbe simplicifolia* hybrids
	Pendulous sedge (*Carex pendula*)		Masterwort (*Astrantia major*)
	Bleeding heart (*Dicentra spectabilis*)		*Hosta* (small-leaved species)
	Hosta (large-leaved species)		Cinnamon fern (*Osmunda cinnamomea*)
	Ostrich fern, shuttlecock fern (*Matteuccia struthiopteris*)		*Pachysandra terminalis*
	Royal fern (*Osmunda regalis*)		*Primula* species
	Rodgersia species		Lungwort (*Pulmonaria* species)
	Thalictrum delavayi		London pride (*Saxifraga* × *urbium*)
5–7 plants per m² (sq yd)	Monkshood (*Aconitum* species)		Turkish comfrey (*Symphytum grandiflorum*)
	Actaea simplex (syn. *Cimicifuga simplex*)		Greater periwinkle (*Vinca major*)
	Lady's mantle (*Alchemilla mollis*)	13–16 plants per m² (sq yd)	Columbine (*Aquilegia* species)
	Japanese anemones (*Anemone hupehensis, A.* × *hybrida*)		Wild ginger (*Asarum europaeum*)
	Astilbe arendsii hybrids		*Dicentra eximia*
	Astilbe thunbergii hybrids		*Epimedium* species
	Bergenia hybrids		Sweet woodruff (*Galium odoratum*)
	Brunnera macrophylla		*Hosta* (small-leaved species)
	Carex morrowii		Yellow archangel (*Lamium galeobdolon*)
	Buckler fern (*Dryopteris* species)		Blue-eyed Mary (*Omphalodes verna*)
	Hellebore (*Helleborus* species)		Sensitive fern (*Onoclea sensibilis*)
	Hosta (medium-leaved species)		Solomon's seal (*Polygonatum* species)
	Himalayan blue poppy (*Meconopsis betonicifolia*)		Foamflower (*Tiarella* species)
	Shield fern (*Polystichum* species)		Woodlily (*Trillium* species)
	Tradescantia Andersonia hybrids		Lesser periwinkle (*Vinca minor*)
			Waldsteinia species
		20–25 plants per m² (sq yd)	Wood anemone (*Anemone nemorosa*)
			Lily-of-the-valley (*Convallaria majalis*)
			Corydalis species
			Dicentra formosa
			Hepatica species

out, and you will need to divide them or thin them out. This is a time-consuming task that you can avoid altogether by planting them at the correct density in the first place (see table on previous page).

A plant's growth habit gives a good indication of how densely it should be planted:

• Plants that put out runners normally spread fast, as do cushion-forming plants.

• Clump-forming plants need rather less space.

• Small plants or plants with only one shoot, such as fox-glove (*Digitalis*), need very little space.

When to plant

It is generally said that con-tainer plants, whether shrubs or perennials, can be planted out at any time of year apart from in winter when the temperature is below freezing. That is to a certain extent true, but it doesn't take into account that success will vary depending on the season.

In the shade, and in particular where new plants are compet-ing with existing shrubs, it's best to confine yourself to the traditional planting seasons of spring and autumn. Autumn

and early spring are the two periods when shrubs and broadleaved trees are in their dormant phase. There is more light at ground level, giving new plants a good start.

Which season you choose for planting is a matter of judge-ment. **Autumn**, for example, is the time when spring-flowering bulbs should be planted out. It also makes sense to combine them with shrubs and perenni-als. In areas that are liable to frosts, new plantings should be protected with leaves or brushwood.

If the soil is very compacted, then it's more sensible to leave it through the winter, when the frost will help to break it up. You can then plant out your perennials in the **spring**, followed by bulbs the following autumn. But if you're planting out in the spring, then you shouldn't hang about. If the plants have already starting sprouting, they will be very sen-sitive indeed, while the young shoots and leaf buds are often very fragile.

If you decide to plant out in the summer, it's important to water regularly during the first year, as this will help the plants to bed in more effectively during the growing season.

How to plant

Once the soil has been prope opened up and prepared (se page 76 ff.), and the surface h been smoothed over with a rake, now is the time to start planting out the items that yc have purchased.

The following tools are needed for this:

• a water trough for soaking plants thoroughly before planting

• knives and secateurs for opening up pots, and for removing any damaged roc or shoots

Any compacted soil should be dug over before planting. This gives it an open structure that will help the plan to take root.

- a long plank to enable you to reach the planting position without compacting the soil unnecessarily
- a trowel and/or a spade for digging out the planting holes
- a rake for smoothing out the soil surface after planting
- a hose or watering can for watering the new plantings.

Now is the time to start preparing your plants. If they are still in their containers, you should first soak them in water for a few hours – although they can manage without this if the weather is exceptionally wet, especially if they have been obtained from the wild. However, roots that are bare of soil will need to be soaked for as long as 24 hours.

Container plants can then be removed from their pots. If the roots are already growing out through the holes in the pot, you will need to cut them back carefully. If the plant has become root-bound, you should loosen the roots by teasing them apart. You need to shorten or remove any long or damaged roots, cutting cleanly to avoid bruising. Any roots that have become badly twisted can also be removed, provided the

resulting wounds aren't too large. This will encourage the growth process and stimulate the formation of new roots, giving your plants a firm hold in the soil.

Your work will also be very much easier if you know what the different plants are once you've planted them all out in the bed.

Place each prepared plant in its intended location, and make a final check to see that it is in the correct position before finally planting out.

Planting perennials

Perennials can be planted out using a trowel.

- Dig out a hole of the same depth as the height of the root ball.
- Loosen the soil around the hole with the trowel to enable the roots to grow better.
- Now place the plant in the hole, checking that the roots are hanging loosely. Fill the gap with soil and press it down around the plant with both hands.
- At this stage the plant should be in the same position relative to the soil surface as when it was still in its pot.

Watch out for weevils!
Weevils like to lay their eggs in loose soil in the shade, where the small white larvae go on to feed on the fleshy roots of plants. Annoyingly, the first thing you may notice is when the plants start to wilt for no apparent reason. This means you have to look very closely at newly bought plants supplied in light composts. Check the root balls very carefully for any weevil larvae – they are about the size of a fingernail. Peat-based and peat-substitute composts are particularly liable to infestation, and should be looked over with extreme care.

- Finally, smooth out the soil and water the plant really thoroughly.
- Within the next fortnight, you should cover the unplanted areas of the bed with a layer of mulch to keep the soil damp and stop weeds from growing.

Planting ground-cover plants

Ground-cover plants should be planted an equal distance apart. At first you should just lay out all the available plants across the area to be planted, and only

Ajuga spreads horizontally, especially in May and June, and if you're not careful it can invade your lawn.

start planting them when you're sure they are placed at regular intervals. They will then grow together without leaving any gaps.

Ground-cover plants have the great advantage of spreading out of their own accord. You can use concrete path edging to stop them spreading over paths, or metal or plastic lawn edging to reduce the chance of them invading the lawn.

You can plant out bulbs until October, but you must store them in cool, dry, dark conditions. Any light tends to make them sprout prematurely, jeopardising their future development. It's sensible to plant them out as soon as possible after you've bought them.

Planting bulbs

Spring-flowering bulbs should be planted out in the shade in September. In the case of a new planting, their position should have been marked out already on the planting plan. With an older planting you could look for gaps to plant in, or else mark out their positions the previous spring. Bulbs should be buried with the flat end at the bottom.

As a general rule of thumb, the **planting depth** should be twice to three times the length of the bulb. Don't allow any air to become trapped underneath the bulb, as this can easily cause the roots to dry out, allowing rot to set in. Finally, fill in the soil above the bulb.

Autumn crocuses (*Colchicum*) are among the autumn-flowering bulbs (corms, strictly speaking). They are sold in the high summer, usually from August onwards, and should be planted out immediately in the same way as spring-flowering bulbs. It will only be a few weeks before the flowers poke out from the soil.

Protecting bulbs from voles

Bluebells (*Hyacinthoides non-scripta*) have fleshy bulbs that

voles are particularly fond of. Protecting them with wire netting is difficult over a large area, and the trick of planting poisonous narcissi nearby can prove ineffective, so alternative methods are called for.

You could try planting the bulbs in large clay pots in a frequented position such as near to the house, as the voles will be unlikely to go there. You can add further protection in the form of close-mesh wire netting at the bottom of each pot and at the surface of the soil. Only when the bluebells begin to sprout will you need to place the pots in the shade or bury them in the soil.

Enabling bulb flowers to grow wild

Scilla (squill) and *Crocus tommasinianus*, like many other spring flowers, look most effective when they are allowed to become naturalised (grow wild), as this gives the planting a certain naturalistic charm.

There are a number of steps you can take in order to speed up this process:

- Don't stint on the number of bulbs you plant. A large bed can take as many as 100 or even 200 bulbs. Simply scatter them over the area and plant them where they fall. This alone will create a natural effect.

• After they've finished flowering, you should always leave the plants to mature. Healthy, living soil will encourage ants and other helpers to spread the seed.

• During the first few years, add some extra bulbs in the autumn. If any clumps form, you can remove these after flowering, and divide and replant the bulbs. The planting will usually become stable after just a few years.

In addition to the two above-mentioned plants, the following will also naturalise well:

• *Galanthus nivalis* (common snowdrop)
• *Anemone blanda*
• *Eranthis hyemalis* (winter aconite)
• *Fritillaria meleagris* (snake's-head fritillary)
• *Cyclamen* species.

Planting trees and shrubs

Trees or shrubs that are to be planted in the shade should always have a firm root ball.

Where tree or shrub roots are wrapped in sacking or a plastic wrapper, the correct planting depth will be obvious from the trunk. The section that was under the soil will be brown, while the areas that were exposed will have a greenish layer of moss and algae.

They may arrive either in containers or with the root ball wrapped in a cloth.

You first need to dig a sufficiently large hole with plenty of loose soil around it. If the soil at the bottom of the hole is heavily compacted, you should mix in some well-rotted garden compost to improve its structure. Then you should pour plenty of water into the hole and allow it to soak in.

Place the root ball in the hole so that it is in the same position relative to the soil surface as it was in the container or in the nursery where the plant came from. If you're planting a large specimen, you can work this out by placing a long cane across the hole. The position of the base of the stem relative to the cane should indicate whether you need to dig deeper or fill up the hole a little before planting.

Snowdrops and Crocus tommasinianus are both plants that naturalise readily. This process is assisted by ants, which carry the seeds with them.

Open up the wrapping and/or any wire around the trunk, and when the root ball is in position, carefully slide the wrapping from beneath the plant.

If the roots are wrapped in sacking, you don't have to remove it – just open it up around the base of the trunk. It is made of perishable material that should decompose within a year of planting.

Finally, fill in the remaining space around the roots with soil, pressing it down with your feet as you go. Press down sufficiently to close up any air pockets without actually compacting the soil.

Use an ericaceous compost if you're planting rhododendrons in a tub. This is also suitable for all moorland or bogland plants, or indeed for any shade plants that like an acid soil.

Leave the soil with a raised edge around where the hole was dug. This will ensure that, when you water your plant, the water will penetrate down to the roots instead of running off to all sides.

Planting rhododendrons

Rhododendrons are very popular as flowering shrubs that are tolerant of shade. The genus *Rhododendron* contains a large number of valuable species and varieties. However, they are generally lime-hating plants that require a very acid soil (i.e. with a low pH value). This means that you not only have to dig a hole, but you have to replace the soil with a potting compost that is more suited to the plant's requirements.

Rhododendron (ericaceous) compost is readily available from garden centres or large DIY stores. Be generous with your quantities so as to allow plenty of room for the roots to grow. Otherwise they will eventually grow out into ordinary garden soil, the increased pH levels will lead to a reduction in the intake of nutrients, and the plant will become weakened and eventually age prematurely.

Inkarho® is the trade name given to new versions of classic rhododendrons that will thrive in neutral soils with a pH value of 6–7, and that will grow even more vigorously in acid soils. (Though not widely sold in the UK yet, they may soon become more readily available.) They are not in fact new varieties of rhododendron, but rather tried and-tested forms that have been grafted onto a new base. If your garden has chalky or lime-rich soil, it will still need to be replaced with a compost that is more suitable for Inkarho® rhododendrons.

Looking at the Tiarella *growing in front of these rhododendron bushes, you can easily see why it is commonly known as foamflower.*

Mulching

As soon as you've finished planting, you will need to cover the soil with a layer of mulch. Mulching fulfils a number of important functions:

• keeping weeds at bay

• preventing the soil from drying out

• encouraging the soil life

• improving soil ventilation

• providing humus and nutrients

• speeding up the warming of the soil.

When planting in the shade, you should look for natural mulches that will provide plenty of humus. Always use well-rotted materials. Fresh clippings will absorb nitrogen as they break down into the soil, depriving the plants of nitrogen. So make sure any clippings are well rotted before using them for mulching.

Leaves mixed with garden compost make a really good mulch. The mixture should be spread generously but evenly around the plants using a spade, then smoothed off with a rake. The mulch layer will get thinner as it breaks down into the soil, so you'll need to top it up about once or twice a year.

Bark mulch has a much higher fibre content than **bark compost**, so will break down much more slowly.

Decorative mulch is made up of particularly attractive pieces of bark with very little fine material. It is very firm and robust, making it an ideal material for paths. It can also be visually very effective if used to divide up plants within a display bed.

Nutrient requirements

Nothing is possible without nutrients, because they are what give plants the strength to grow, bloom and fruit. Spring-flowering bulbs, for example, need to have plenty of nutrients available during the flowering season, because this is when they produce seed while at the same time storing up energy for next year's flowers. Further energy is stored in the bulbs in the form of starch, which will be used to kick-start the early spring growth. Trees, shrubs and perennials need enough nutrients to enable them to sprout in the spring, and further nutrients must be available for the development of shoots, leaves and flowers.

Bark mulch protects the soil and makes for easy-care plantings, and can also look very attractive.

Different types of fertiliser

Fertilisers can be variously categorised according to where they come from and how they function:

• **Organic fertilisers** are made up of decomposed animal and plant matter. They can be made from algae, stinging nettles or indeed any decaying plant matter – garden compost, for example. In the soil, the constituent elements are gradually converted into a form which the plants can absorb. The process is therefore a very slow one. These slow-release fertilisers are the

Foxgloves are typical biennial plants. A leaf rosette is formed in the first year, followed by the flowers the following year. However, if you cut them back after flowering, another flower stem will appear in the following season.

most important for use with shade plants.

- **Mineral fertilisers** are either extracted from the ground or produced by chemical means. Being water-soluble, they are immediately available to the plants, making them ideal for kick-starting growth in the early spring.
- **NPK fertilisers** are mineral fertilisers that contain the three main plant nutrients in specific proportions (see table below). The exact proportions can be geared to the particular requirements of the plants. Growmore is a typical NPK fertiliser.
- **Long-term fertilisers** include both slow-release and controlled-release fertilisers. The latter are covered with a special coating that releases the fertiliser in response to the soil temperature. Although very expensive, these fertilisers are particularly effective when used with shade plants.

Working the soil

Looking after the soil is at least as important as planting. The best basis for healthy plant growth is humus-rich soil with an open structure that enables the roots to spread out effectively.

Turning over the soil

In the shade, the soil rarely dries out completely, and this combined with the high humus content means that little work is actually required in this area. However, you may need to use a rake for adding fertiliser or compost.

This is usually no problem except in the case of ground-cover plants or perennials with shallow roots. The roots of certain plants such as Japanese anemones, *Astilbe* or wild ginger (*Asarum europaeum*) spread out only a few centimetres below the surface, so loosening up the soil will destroy the young shoots.

Fertiliser nutrients		
Main nutrients	**Functions**	**Organic fertilisers that contain them**
Nitrogen (N)	necessary for leaf growth	hoof and horn, green fertiliser
Phosphorus (P)	involved in flower and fruit formation	bonemeal, pigeon droppings
Potassium (K)	involved in cell formation; improves disease-resistance	wood ashes

Adding humus

Humus needs to be added to mature clumps of perennials. This is to stop the roots pushing upwards and lying flat along the ground, the effect of which is to reduce growth by starving the plants of nutrients.

Adding humus can also mean that you no longer need to remove and divide perennials (see next page), or at the very least it can enable you to postpone that particular job for a few years.

The best material for providing humus is well-rotted garden compost. The following plants need extra humus in the autumn or spring:

- *Actaea* (syn. *Cimicifuga*) species and varieties
- Japanese anemone (*Anemone hupehensis*, *A.* × *hybrida*)
- *Astilbe* species and varieties
- alum root (*Heuchera* hybrids).

Pruning requirements vary

In general, wilted flowers should be removed from a plant unless you want it to self-seed or it will later produce decorative fruits. The flower heads

Herbaceous perennials should be cut back in the autumn, but you should always wait until the flowers have lost all their beauty. There's no point in spoiling their appearance by cutting back too early.

should be cut back sufficiently so that the cut stem is hidden by foliage.

In the case of some herbaceous perennials, radical pruning is recommended after flowering has finished. Lady's mantle (*Alchemilla mollis*) and *Geranium endressii* flowers look particularly attractive on new growth, for example. Individual plants can be cut back virtually to ground level using a hedge-trimmer. Afterwards it's advisable (though not absolutely necessary) to spread some garden compost around the plants.

Border plants or ground-cover plants that have spread over a large area can even be trimmed with a lawnmower and the leaves raked together afterwards. The following ground-

The plants named above aren't the only ones that benefit from extra humus. You could give your ground-cover plants a similar treat in the autumn or in the early spring before the new growth begins. A layer of finely crumbled garden compost will give them extra strength and also encourage the soil fauna.

The gently curved shoots of Solomon's seal (Polygonatum) *look very attractive either side of these steps. This plant develops very slowly, which means it should never be divided.*

Dividing perennials

Early spring is the time to divide clumps of perennials that have become too large for their own good. You can usually tell from the plants themselves when this needs to be done, as they start to become weak and reluctant to flower.

The whole plant should be dug up, and a section removed for replanting. Smaller plants can be divided with a knife, though if they have become heavily matted it might be easier with a spade. Divided sections for replanting should each be approximately the size of a fist, with just a few new shoots visible. These are usually to be found around the edges of the clump.

If there is no room in your garden for the rest of the clump, you could share it out among neighbours or friends.

The following shade plants should be divided after two to four years:

- *Aster divaricatus*
- primrose and oxlip (*Primula veris* and *P. elatior* hybrids).

The following plants should be divided after six to eight years:

- monkshood (*Aconitum* species)

cover plants are suitable for the lawnmower treatment:

- *Euphorbia amygdaloides* var. *robbiae*
- *Geranium endressii*
- rose of Sharon (*Hypericum calycinum*)
- lilytuft (*Liriope muscari*)
- greater periwinkle (*Vinca major*)
- *Pachysandra terminalis*.

Herbaceous perennials should be cut back in the autumn when they have lost all their beauty (i.e. when their autumn colouring is over). Otherwise the wet leaves will lie on top of the plants, encouraging rot and providing the ideal winter refuge for slugs and snails.

The dried-up stems and fern fronds can look quite attractive among the various evergreen plants, and you can then wait until the early spring to cut these remnants down to the ground to make way for new growth.

In the case of early-flowering Lenten roses (*Helleborus orientalis* hybrids), you should remove the old leaves to allow the new flowers to attain their full glory. *Epimedium* and *Bergenia* hybrids should similarly be cleared for flowering, with the removal of old or unsightly leaves.

Trees and shrubs should be pruned just as the new shoots begin to stir. In the winter a little thinning may be needed to prevent the undergrowth from becoming too heavily shaded. This can usually be done at intervals of two or three years.

common snowdrop
(*Galanthus nivalis*)

clump-forming types of
Geranium (*G. × magnificum*
and *G. phaeum*)

- hellebore and Christmas rose
(*Helleborus* species)

- bluebell (*Hyacinthoides non-
scripta*)

- globeflower (*Trollius*
hybrids).

The following shade plants
should never be divided:

- *Cyclamen coum*

- bleeding heart (*Dicentra
spectabilis*)

- umbrella plant (*Darmera
peltata*)

- Solomon's seal (*Polygonatum* species).

A healthy garden
without pesticides

In any garden, and especially in
an ornamental garden, it should
be possible to manage without
pesticides.

The best basis for healthy
plant growth is the right choice
of plants for each particular
location. A further important
factor is the right balance of
nutrients – because too much
fertiliser can be just as damaging as too little.

The plants should never be
allowed to become too dense.
The leaves will not dry out
properly, which will encourage
fungal infections, and the
damage from leaves rubbing
together provides easy access
for pests and diseases. Planting
a wide variety of species will
prevent any diseases from
spreading too far, and will also
attract a greater variety of beneficial insects.

It pays to know plenty about
the various diseases and pests
so that you can help the plants
to combat them effectively.
Small populations of pests are
in fact healthy, as these activate
the plants' defence mechanisms
and also attract the creatures
that feed on the pests.

And if a plant does become
diseased and die, then it's
worth remembering how difficult it was in the first place to
choose from so many different
plants. It means you now have
the opportunity to plant a new
and different bulb or perennial
in its place.

Typical problems in the
shade

Because most shade plantings
are based on naturalistic designs
made up of many different

species, they are vulnerable to
only a few really serious pests
and diseases. These are
described below, together with
typical symptoms and ways to
combat them.

Hellebore leaf blotch

This disease is caused by a
fungus that is likely to attack
Helleborus species when they
are growing in the shade. It
takes the form of brownish-
black spots that spread inwards
from the edges of the leaves. In
severe cases the stems and
flowers are affected too.

As the plants are weakened by
black spot, it should be dealt
with immediately by removing
all affected parts and disposing
of them together with the
domestic waste.

The spores are actually spread
during the summer, which
means it's important to take
preventative measures in the
early spring before they get a
chance to develop. You could

One way to ward off slugs is to add
some clippings of culinary sage to
the mulch. This will produce a scent
that slugs find unpleasant. The
essential oils from the sage are also
beneficial to plant growth.

Slugs are particularly partial to the shade because the moisture is retained there.

check the pH level of the soil and make adjustments to bring it into line with the plant's requirements. Fertilisers with too much nitrogen will also make plants more liable to infection.

Slugs and snails

Slugs and snails have a special liking for soft young shoots. Every gardener must have lost at least one plant, whether a *Hosta* or a *Ligularia*, to the ravages of these creatures. It is important to understand slugs and snails, and special precautions are required in the shade given that they are so fond of dark, damp places.

There are various ways of dealing with slugs and snails:

• Don't choose any plants that are vulnerable to attack – or

rather avoid anything with particularly soft shoots such as *Dicentra*. If you want to plant *Hosta*, choose one of the more slug-resistant forms (see page 23). And always avoid *Ligularia dentata* 'Desdemona' at all costs, as this plant seems to attract them.

• Provide special places with exactly the right conditions for slugs and snails, and remove them regularly. The damp hollows beneath planks, stones or empty grapefruit halves make ideal winter refuges where they can lay their eggs. Collecting them isn't everyone's cup of tea, but you'll be glad to be rid of them. Rubber gloves are recommended for the task. If you're not happy killing them with salt or boiling water, you could always carry them away to some nearby woodland.

• Protect the young shoots in the spring by making life uncomfortable for these greedy litle creatures. Their soft bodies are sensitive to anything sharp, which they will avoid if you spread it around the plant – sharp sand, for instance, or pine

needles or sawdust. Or you could take cuttings of sharp-edged grasses such as reeds and add them to the mulch. You'll need to be careful not to leave any gaps, however, because slugs are as greedy as they are small, and will quickly discover any breaches in the defences.

Weevils

Weevils cause two types of damage. Firstly, the adult insects chew around the edges of rhododendron leaves, spoiling their symmetrical shape. Secondly, and much more seriously, the larvae eat the roots of perennials, sometimes consuming them completely so that the plant withers and dies.

There are only two ways of dealing with weevils in beds and borders: extreme care when buying and planting out (see page 81), and biological

Weevil larvae are extremely partial to fleshy roots.

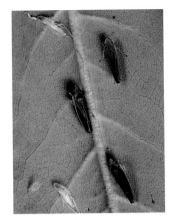

Rhododendron leafhoppers do their damage in the summer, when these red-and-green insects can be found on the leaves in the early hours of the morning.

ontrols. The latter take the orm of predatory eelworms nematodes) that can be added) the watering can. If an infes- ation occurs, treatment should e carried out regularly from 1ay through to September. The dult weevils are nocturnal, so an be removed from rhodo- endron leaves after dark.

Rhododendron leafhoppers
ny infestation will become pparent in the spring, when he thick flower buds turn rown and fall off the shoots. lowever, the attack will have ctually occurred the previous ummer, when these insects njected their eggs inside the buds, at the same time infecting hem with fungal spores that vill eventually kill off the bud. a bad infestation will greatly educe flowering in the ollowing spring.

Rhododendron leafhoppers ave striking red-and-green olouring, and can be found on he leaves in the early morning. ll affected buds should be completely removed. Some of he leafhoppers can be caught by means of sticky yellow traps, which can be hung up in the early summer. However, such methods may be blessed with only limited success.

By far the most effective remedy is to encourage strong growth by providing all the right nutrients, because it is the old or weak bushes that the leafhoppers go for.

Variegated leaves turn green
It sometimes happens that the leaves on variegated forms of plants turn uniformly green. If the whole plant is affected, then one can assume that it is in too dark a location, and that the pale areas of the leaves are turn- ing green in order to increase photosynthesis and improve the plant's metabolism. The only remedy is to move the plant to a less shady position. Variegat- ed forms of *Hosta* and ivy (*Hedera*) are particularly liable to turn green from lack of light.

at a glance

- The basis for success in the shade is matching the plants to the conditions. You need to work out the light and soil conditions exactly in order to be able to decide on the right plants to choose and/or improve the conditions before planting.

- An open, humus-rich soil provides the ideal starting conditions for a new planting.

- It's important to leave enough space between plants so that the young plants can spread out nicely without impinging on each other's space.

- A good layer of mulch reduces the maintenance requirements, and adds humus and nutrients to the soil.

- There are only a few pests and diseases that cause problems in the shade, and these can be dealt with by biological means and/or simple removal.

Index